A volume in the series

MASTERS of MODERN LANDSCAPE DESIGN

JAMES ROSE

A VOICE OFFSTAGE

DEAN CARDASIS

THE UNIVERSITY OF GEORGIA PRESS
ATHENS

LIBRARY OF AMERICAN LANDSCAPE HISTORY
AMHERST, MASSACHUSETTS

To Liz, Lily Rose, Maggie, Louie, Stephanie, and Lucy, with love.

Publication of this book was made possible in part by the
Bruce and Georgia McEver Fund for the Arts and Environment.

Published by the University of Georgia Press, Athens, Georgia 30602
www.ugapress.org
in association with Library of American Landscape History

Designed and typeset by Jonathan D. Lippincott
Set in Bembo and Avenir
Printed and bound by Four Colour Print Group

The paper in this book meets the guidelines for
permanence and durability of the Committee on
Production Guidelines for Book Longevity of the
Council on Library Resources.

Printed in Korea
17   18   19   20   21   P   5   4   3   2   1

Library of Congress Control Number: 2016955478

ISBN: 9780820350950 (paperback: alk. paper)

Frontispiece: Rose at work in West Orange, NJ, 1952.
Courtesy James Rose Center.

SERIES FUNDERS

Ann and Clayton Wilhite
Ann Arbor Area Community Foundation

Dede Delaney and James R. Turner
Blackhaw Fund—Impact Assets

Nancy R. Turner
Viburnum Trilobum Fund—New York Community Trust

VOLUME FUNDERS

Foundation for Landscape Studies

Michael Van Valkenburgh, FASLA
Michael Van Valkenburgh Associates

Reed Hilderbrand, LLC

Cornelia Oberlander, FCSLA, FASLA

Peter Walker, FASLA
PWP Landscape Architecture

Jeff Allen, ASLA
Jeff Allen Landscape Architecture

Keith LeBlanc, FASLA
Leblanc Jones Landscape Architects

Lauren and Stephen Stimson, FASLA
Stimson Associates

R. Bruce Stephenson

Robert A. M. Stern
Robert A. M. Stern Architects

CONTENTS

PREFACE

James Rose's (1913–1991) singular approach to landscape design was grounded in a sense of the garden as theater and the designer as playwright. "In the backstage of his mind," Rose wrote, "[the landscape architect] knows full well he cannot invent characters or situations to his liking but must deal with both—as they are; it is often in that fine line between what is and what it pretends to be that the landscape drama takes its shape." Rose's methods were distinctive in other ways, too, especially in his prescient commitment to environmental integrity, evidenced by the frugal use (and reuse) of found materials and close attention to existing site conditions, and his celebration of the garden as a continually evolving entity. "The metamorphosis is seen minute by minute, season by season, year by year, " Rose wrote in 1987. "Through this looking glass, 'finish' is another word for death."

Playful, often contentious, highly intellectual yet deeply

spiritual, Rose navigated the social and artistic currents of midcentury America and his own turbulent personality to create some of the most serene yet emotionally stirring gardens of his time. Despite Rose's focus on the present moment—in his later years, he became a Zen Buddhist—he took steps to preserve his own home and garden as a study center, the James Rose Center for Landscape Architectural Research and Design in Ridgewood, New Jersey. Serving as the Center's director since it was established, Dean Cardasis, who knew Rose well, has worked tirelessly to stabilize this exceptional place. From this experience and his insights into Rose's writings and other built work, Cardasis writes with authority and a sometimes wry perspective not unlike his subject's.

In the late 1930s Rose began publishing on modernist space composition, buoyed by the "revolution" he and others were inciting against the Beaux-Arts methods of an earlier generation. These influential articles were followed by others equally thoughtful, and eventually four books. Cardasis discusses these theoretical (and theatrical) musings as well as Rose's methods, which were highly improvisatory. Throughout, he illuminates Rose's sense of house and garden as a single, integrated entity. "He called these fusions of house and garden 'space-sculptures-with-shelters,'" Cardasis writes. "A 'house' was not an isolated object decorated with landscaping but merely the sheltered part of a larger landscape space, originating from the extant conditions of its site."

Most of Rose's built work has been changed beyond recognition in the years since his death, owing to its subtlety and, to some degree, ephemeralness. Cardasis's book, the first on this distinctive modernist, is thus an especially welcome addition to the literature and to the Masters of Modern

Landscape Design series. By illuminating an almost-vanished body of work by one of the midcentury's most original landscape architects, Cardasis significantly expands our understanding of an important and understudied period in the history of American landscape design. Students, historians, landscape architects, and even home gardeners struggling to enliven the blandness of suburbia will find Rose's biography thought-provoking, as well as informative.

I thank Dean Cardasis for bringing this project to LALH, and I am deeply grateful to the editors who worked with him to develop it over many years: in the final stages, Carol Betsch and Arthur Johnson, and from the beginning, Sarah Allaback, who also helped assemble the illustration program. Jonathan Lippincott designed the book, and Allaback created the index. Funders to the series and the volume are listed on page v. My profound thanks to all of them and to our colleagues at the University of Georgia Press.

Robin Karson
Executive Director
Library of American Landscape History

ACKNOWLEDGMENTS

My thanks to the owners of the James Rose designed projects I visited in preparing this book, for graciously opening their homes and sharing their stories. These include Richard Van Ness, Millicent Anisfield, Florence Paley, Sidney and Rebecca Yarbrough, Madeline Tremaine, Lois and Carol Macht, Gordon Borteck and Cheryl Rubin, Mary Keith Averett, and Nancy Goodell. My thanks also to Sarah Allaback, for her critical reading and thoughtful suggestions. Rose's legacy would have been lost, and any book on him rendered impossible, without the enthusiasm and hard work of my students and interns at the James Rose Center. Although they are too numerous to list, their importance in preserving Rose's legacy cannot be understated. I also acknowledge the significant role of my own teacher, Joseph Volpe, whose comprehensive landscape spatial pedagogy helped roll back the curtain between Rose's world and my own. Lastly, I owe a great debt to Elizabeth Thompson, who was my full partner in uncovering Rose and establishing the James Rose Center, and without whom little would have been possible.

JAMES ROSE

OVERVIEW

Prologue

In the late spring of 1989, I was outside Hills North, home of the University of Massachusetts's landscape architecture program, waiting for James Rose to arrive. My generation of designers had lost track of Rose, arguably the most rebellious of the trio of landscape designers—Rose, Daniel Urban Kiley, and Garrett Eckbo—who had ushered the profession (kicking and screaming) into the modern era in the mid-to-late 1930s (fig. 1). The other two designers had stayed in the public eye, executing significant private, public, and corporate work for over fifty years—work that helped define the modern era in landscape architecture—but Rose, whose early writings on landscape space were so incisive, seemed to have fallen off the face of the earth. I had heard that he'd been designing gardens in New Jersey when my colleague Elizabeth Thompson found him and we conspired to have him visit our school.

Fig. 1. Rose, c. 1937. Photograph courtesy Arlene Eckbo.

As I was imagining the enigmatic designer, a rusty, egg-yolk-colored 1970s VW van pulled up. The passenger door opened, and a small man stepped down onto the fake brick courtyard. His shoes were old and worn through. His blue-and-green plaid pants clashed with an alternate plaid shirt.

An incredibly long, almost wizard-like straw hat grazed his shoulders and shaded his face. As he looked up I could see he was wearing glasses, but one frame was empty, and the remaining one held a tinted sunglass lens. In that instant I had my first silent lesson from the iconoclastic modern landscape architect James Rose: "Have no preconceptions."

As I learned more about Rose and his work, I came to recognize some of the reasons he was not better known, as well as to feel the importance of helping to bring his legacy to light. Rose was elusive and difficult to get close to—an uncompromising, highly individual, and often contentious person whom one writer referred to as the "James Dean of landscape architecture."[1] He never graduated from high school, yet he managed to enroll in agriculture courses at Cornell University and then transfer from there to Harvard University's newly established Graduate School of Design, from which he was summarily expelled for refusing to design in the prescribed Beaux-Arts style. He got into a fistfight with James Thurber at a cocktail party in New York just seconds after meeting him, and he unleashed an attack dog (a German shepherd that Rose had named Mr. Hyde) on members of the Museum of Modern Art's board of directors while interviewing for a job on Long Island. (He didn't get the job.) He took LSD with Timothy Leary (and wondered what the fuss was all about) and studied Zen with Alan Watts before angrily renouncing Watts. He drank too much, drove too fast, and argued too vehemently. Yet he made serene and contemplative gardens—"space-sculptures," he called them—and wrote not only sharp and penetrating criticism but also eloquent and even poetic descriptions of garden and landscape.

In the latter part of his career Rose worked directly on-site, spontaneously improvising with the landscape in a manner more like Jack Kerouac or Charlie Parker than the

Olmsted Brothers or EDAW. Such a method failed to produce plans that could be disseminated to the general public, further contributing to Rose's anonymity, but it resulted in gardens that possessed a unique vitality for those lucky enough to experience them. Rose's persistent focus on the spatial, spiritual, and ecological nature of private gardens at a time when the post–World War II design imagination was more readily captured by shopping centers and corporate headquarters was characteristically out of step, and his work became less well recognized. In a burgeoning suburban landscape of houses with useless front lawns and decorative foundation plantings (which Rose once referred to as looking like "parsley at the base of a turkey"),ecological gardens of space and light were almost invisible.[2]

By the late 1980s, a growing interest in constructing more environmentally sustainable places had begun to align with Rose's perception of suburbia as a spiritual and ecological wasteland, thus making his private gardens more relevant to a contemporary audience (though they were still largely unknown). And I discovered that other obstacles to better understanding Rose had become opportunities. Private gardens are often short-lived, but many of his recent ones—including Rose's magnum opus, his home in Ridgewood, New Jersey—still existed (fig. 2). Not only could these gardens be experienced in person, but they also could be studied and documented. Although Rose was in his mid-seventies when I met him, he was still lively, sharp, and energetic—at once dismissive yet eager to talk if you were serious about design. And the fact that he had written so incisively about his gardens and about modern landscape design (despite his seemingly paradoxical mistrust of words) provided a distinctive complement to his built works, which could help immeasurably in understanding him.

Fig. 2. Rose house and northern courtyard, 1954. Photograph by Lionel Freedman.

As a curious young designer I got to know Rose better over the next two years, before his death in 1991, and in some ways even more so in subsequent years as I helped to establish the James Rose Center for Landscape Architectural Research and Design, rehabilitating Rose's home, documenting his most recent projects, and gaining access to his revealing, if minimal, personal and professional records. Rose's contempt for the relevance of biographical facts and the futility of what he called "the influence game" inspired me to try to focus on his work and ideas and to tell his story, to some extent, in his own words. His keen observations, insightful critique of his times, and revealing letters, as well as the imaginative personal stories about the postwar American suburbs that are found in his books, are as much a part of his artistic production as the built works. Accordingly, I have let Rose speak for himself throughout the book, sometimes at length.

In some ways Rose's story is simply that of a gifted person trying to find harmony with modern times, but between the lines it may also be read as the story of those times themselves, written in a life lived as a creative protest against them.

Introduction

James Rose is best known as one of three Harvard students who rebelled against their Beaux-Arts training in the 1930s, propelling the profession of landscape architecture into the modern era.[3] Rose himself did so largely through the production of nineteen incisive articles written in a three-year span between 1938 and 1941, particularly a series of essays for *Pencil Points* (later *Progressive Architecture*), as well as another series for *California Arts and Architecture* and a three-part essay for *Architectural Record* that Rose coauthored with Garrett Eckbo and Dan Kiley.[4] In these articles Rose helps define a new vision for landscape architecture, rebuts the claims of the profession's arrière-garde that it need not modernize, calls out modern architecture's failure to address the landscape as a place for modern living, and promotes ideas about a new form of landscape space, using photographs of his own three-dimensional landscape models as illustrations.

Late in his life, a cynical Rose rejected others' characterization of him as a leader in landscape architecture's modern movement. "I'm no missionary," he'd often protest. "I do what pleases me."[5] And what pleased Rose for most of the postwar era was to explore an alternative vision of the American Dream while residing in Ridgewood, an affluent suburb of New York City (fig. 3). In four wry, satirical books (*Creative Gardens*, 1958;

Fig. 3. Rose hosting a party in the northern courtyard of his home, 1954.
Courtesy James Rose Center (JRC).

Gardens Make Me Laugh, 1965; *Modern American Gardens—Designed by James Rose*, 1967; and *The Heavenly Environment—A Landscape Drama in Three Acts with a Backstage Interlude*, 1987), as well as in built works executed between 1941 and 1991, he mocked (and proposed alternatives to) the suburban landscape of culverts, parking lots, and "precious object" houses that was destroying the natural environment and producing what he saw as a banal and dysfunctional quality of life.

Rose's first postwar gardens were radical yet commonsense. His "modular gardens," "gardens without houses," and "space-sculptures-with-shelters" deployed traditional and unique materials in original ways to create seamless modern landscape space for American family living (fig. 4).[6] Increasingly, Rose's gardens became more spiritual and were characterized by direct, spontaneous improvisation with the land. Rose abhorred waste and made his gardens out of found

Fig. 4. Mineola, NY, garden, 1953. Photograph by Ezra Stoller. © Ezra Stoller/Esto.

objects, native plants, and recycled materials and constructions that were originally intended for other purposes, as well as whatever he could scavenge from the sites themselves. "I'd much rather do something extraordinary with the common-place," he once quipped, "than something common with the extraordinary."[7] Old doors became elegant garden benches, metal barbeques were turned into fountains, and leftover roof flashing morphed into sculptural lanterns within the larger space-sculptures that were the gardens. His gardens preserved and engaged rather than ignored (or utterly destroyed) their sites' existing biological and geophysical features and systems, as existing trees, rock outcroppings, and other features, along with scavenged railroad ties and other salvaged materials, were employed in a constantly changing, spontaneous, flexible, obtuse-angled, asymmetrical spatial geometry.

Rose's gardens reflected the creative and spatial nature of modern times in ways that were more efficient and less wasteful of resources than the designs of his contemporaries, thus incorporating a conservation ethic into a modern design aesthetic. But Rose's designs did more than presage our interest today in "green" design. He had an acute awareness of the fundamental role of space in provoking people's perception of nature, and he designed environmentally sensitive gardens in such a way as to heighten that perception, making his gardens vehicles for contemplation and self-discovery. With space folded and locked into its defining materials, his gardens are like giant, almost transparent origami, encouraging a fusion of the self with nature to unfold as one moved within them.

In 1960 Rose was invited to participate in the first World Design Conference (WoDeCo) in Tokyo, Japan. This experience led to an appreciation of Japanese culture that would continue throughout his life and that he would integrate into his design approach.[8] Because of this influence, his work has sometimes been mislabeled "Japanese," but few things affronted him more than the accusation that he was making Japanese gardens. Once, in response to a query from a prospective New Jersey client as to whether he could create a Japanese garden for her, he replied, "Of course. Whereabouts in Japan do you live?"[9] That kind of response to what he would call his clients' "mind fixes" was characteristic of James Rose. But on examination, Rose was often saying more than met the ear, and if a client was willing to search for the meaning *between* the lines, the adventure could begin. Rose realized that in the way he responded to clients, just as in the way he responded to sites, he was already working on their gardens. And while he never met a site he couldn't love, he rejected more commissions than he accepted, dismissing most prospective clients as hopeless. Of course, Rose's often uncen-

Fig. 5. Klaiman garden, rock assemblage, Saddle River, NJ, 1992. Photograph by author. Courtesy JRC.

sored condemnation caused many of his prospective clients to reject him as well, but Rose asserted that such rejections suited him just fine. When a client was able to accept the challenge of the adventure Rose presented, the result was a distinctive modern American garden that was a portrait—Rose would say "mirror"—of the client and his or her site (fig. 5).

From 1944 until his death in 1991, as Rose was satirizing suburbia in his books and creating distinctive gardens, he designed, built, lived in, and perpetually reinvented his home in Ridgewood. Elizabeth K. Meyer described Rose's home as "a vision of the ideal minimalist residence built as a critique of post–World War II suburban planning and design conventions," and Peter Walker praised it as "one of the most important designs of the last half-century."[10] At heart, it was also a constantly changing expression of Rose's need to

Fig. 6. James Rose Center, 1996. Photograph by Frederick Charles. © fcharles.com.

maintain his equilibrium in what he perceived as a corrupt and destructive suburbia (fig. 6).

A New Mental Atmosphere

> A friend of mine had inherited a farm in Pennsylvania, and she asked me to do the landscape. A charming old place in the hills, it had orchards and old stone walls, and a magnificent view across the valley. With a fireplace in every room and a great lawn that swept down to the view, with gnarled apple trees spotted here and there, it was everyone's dream of a house. I had lived in just such a house as a child, and in the same community and I knew the life that centered around it. What is more important, I knew how it *felt* to live in such a place. I knew both the virtues and the faults. I understood the pleasant sense of family life held together by its closeness to the soil and its remoteness from distractions, the good things like a cellar full of preserves and a warm kitchen with food that has never tasted quite the same anywhere since. And then the other things like the smothered sensation you get when you first realize that the world is large. —James Rose, 1940[11]

It is hard to escape the conclusion that a desire to resolve the tension between his early rural life along the Delaware River, less than seventy-five miles from New York City, and the beckoning of the larger world led Rose to become a landscape architect. He suggested as much when reflecting on his choice of landscape architecture (as opposed to city planning or architecture) as his area of study upon admission to Harvard's Graduate School of Design in 1936.[12] Rose's solitary years in rural America, with its complementary ethos of mistrust for institutions and belief in nature and the individual, were steeped in an American transcendentalist tradition that remained with him throughout his life.[13] Rose's idyllic time in rural Pennsylvania was short-lived, however, as his world enlarged first to Paterson, New Jersey, where his family had moved by the time he was seven, and then, after his father's death, to New York City, where he attended DeWitt Clinton High School.[14] Still, the family retained the Pennsylvania property throughout his life, and he, his mother, Mirna (Minnie), and two sisters, Jean Gillmor and Virginia Rose, often returned there.

Rose found tremendous stimulation in the new ideas and myriad artistic expressions he encountered in the galleries, museums, and theaters in and around New York City in the late 1920s and early to mid-1930s, even as he dealt with poverty, living much of the time just before and during the Great Depression in a household with no real wage earner. On reflection, Rose generally considered "modernism" as growing out of the Industrial Revolution, the global shift to democracy, quantum physics, and the theory of relativity.[15] And while he certainly would have cringed at any attempt to characterize the spirit of these times through specific "influences" on him, as one who wrote insightfully about modern art and culture Rose might have agreed that his work is better understood in the context of the arts and sciences that contributed to the zeitgeist he experienced. As he described it in 1938: "Contemporary design represents a change in kind, a change in conception, the expression of a new mentality we have derived from the effects of the industrial and economic revolutions. These revolutions have the significance for our civilization that the discoveries of Galileo, Copernicus, and Magellan had for the Renaissance. They have put a transparent but impenetrable screen between us and the past, and we find ourselves in a new mental atmosphere."[16]

Rose was born on March 23 (Easter Sunday), 1913, amid

intensely changing times in the arts and sciences. A radical break from past scientific thought was emerging, exemplified by Albert Einstein's theories of relativity and Sigmund Freud's theories of the subconscious mind. The concept that space and time are relative, as well as the idea that primal impulses and counterbalancing restrictions subconsciously provoke our thoughts and actions, paralleled the expressions of modern artists in what quickly proliferated into numerous critical subdivisions within the modern idiom. Cubists explored multiple, simultaneous points of view on flat, two-dimensional surfaces. Dadaists redefined the meaning of ordinary things, flaunting tradition and convention and championing an anarchistic view in which it might be said that the only rule was that there *were* no rules. Constructivists addressed the fluency between concrete space and ethereal mass in three-dimensional constructions and sculptures. Surrealists explored the world of dreams and of the subconscious. They were revolutionaries. They published artistic manifestos extolling their individual points of view.

Despite apparent divisions, the lines were not so clearly drawn between the various modern "isms." During the first third of the twentieth century, many painters and sculptors moved away from representation and toward abstraction; away from a sensibility focused on romantic and Victorian ideals of "Nature" and toward one that engaged with and even celebrated twentieth-century urban industrial life; away from the sentimental past and toward an ideal and rational future. As the contemporary art critic Kim Levin has summarized, art of the modernist period "was experimental: the creation of new forms was its task. . . . [It] had the logic of structure, the logic of dreams, the logic of gesture or material. It longed for perfection and demanded purity, clarity, order. And it denied everything else, especially the past:

idealistic, ideological, and optimistic, modernism was predicated on the glorious future, the new and improved."[17]

For many, arriving at "the new and improved" involved removing all that had been previously accepted. As if to discover what remained beneath the layers of no longer relevant musical forms, Igor Stravinsky in his *Rites of Spring* (1913) gave voice to the subconscious, expressing atonal and rhythmically primitive organizations of sound that were apparently ordered by gut feelings rather than by established structural conventions. Writers such as James Joyce and William Faulkner invented new literary forms driven by excursions into the mind and by new conceptions of time and consciousness. By the 1930s, Ezra Pound's exhortation to "make it new" had become a call to arms for a generation of artists and writers for whom previous forms were irrelevant. The modernist poet and physician William Carlos Williams, in his conception of a measure based on the minimalist "breath unit," sought to distill language to its essence. In his well-known haiku-like poem "The Red Wheelbarrow" (1923), Williams rejects all nonessential words and formal and metric conventions in poetry to create an authentic American image/language. In the process, he stresses the importance of the ordinary, overlooked things in the world:

so much depends
upon

a red wheel
barrow

glazed with rain
water

beside the white
chickens[18]

As Rose became aware of works of modern art and literature through independent reading and visits to the galleries and museums in and around New York, the stimulating atmosphere must have provided relief from that "smothered sensation" he experienced in his childhood along the Delaware. In its tendency to think (and create) abstractly; its conception of complex, nonlineal space and time; its respect for the subconscious; its passion for the essential; its appreciation for the commonplace and ordinary; and its general rebelliousness against convention, the modern mentalité inspired Rose. His experiences in New York set the stage for his participation in the modern revolution in landscape architecture after he arrived at Harvard in 1936, and they continued to provide an intellectual framework for all of his subsequent production.

But of all the art forms Rose encountered in New York, theater played a unique and major role, bringing out a dramatic sensibility that would come to infuse just about everything in his life.[19] His continuing enthusiasm for the theater is apparent in a letter he sent his mother from Ithaca, after leaving New York City to attend Cornell:

If this thrilling dramatic season does not close soon you will find me going to Columbia instead of Cornell. Now, you simply must follow my orders: the next time you go to New York get tickets for both "Cherry Orchard" and "Alice in Wonderland" at the New Amsterdam Theater (42nd St.) and then see what you can do for tickets to see "Design for Living" (at least this one), "Alien Corn," and "Biography." Our vacation begins April 1 and ends April 10; I probably will not be able to get home until Monday the 3rd or Tuesday the 4th, but if you wrote that you had the tickets for tomorrow night, I would start walking right now.[20]

Developments in architecture and, to a lesser degree, landscape architecture also contributed to the new mental atmosphere. Rose himself wrote observantly about the merits and shortcomings of both fields, often using modern art and literature as touchstones. In its elimination of ornament and in the aesthetic expression of the structural logic of buildings, one can see a parallel between modern architecture and the stripped-down structure of Williams's poem, with buildings aspiring to be as unadorned, clear, and simple as that red wheelbarrow. Similarly, in its conception of and obsession with open or free space that was "defined" rather than enclosed, one can see a parallel to the abstract spatial explorations of constructivist sculptors such as Naum Gabo, as well as to the intellectual constructs of modern science. Paradoxically, as buildings became simpler and clearer expressions of their structures, the interior spaces they described became more complex and ambiguous.

From Rose's viewpoint, modern architects' idea of free and open space was also chained to a totally unacceptable romantic conception of the landscape as wilderness. Frank Lloyd Wright, whom Rose admired in many ways, initiated the idea of the open plan in architecture as an expression of a "freer" organization of space. Like Rose, Wright valued a personal experience of nature. Unlike Rose, Wright saw nature as something not to be messed with—except within the construction footprint of his buildings. In Wright's conception of "organic architecture," furnishings and buildings are harmoniously integrated with the landscape. With their general horizontality and open floor plans, Wright's Prairie style houses reflected the openness and horizontality of the Midwest. Later, Wright became more concerned with relating each building to the natural conditions of its particular site. Indeed, Wright often referred to buildings as being like trees, rooted in and growing from their sites.

Wright's plastic, open spatial expression within his buildings provided an analogue to the mythic "natural" landscapes from which the buildings arose and into which their spaces often flowed. However, as Rose noted, Wright did not make any attempt to design the landscapes just outside his buildings: "Wright, himself, had the great gift of making the landscape inseparable from his buildings to a degree probably equaled by no other architect of this century or in any country and which most have not even approached. . . . Wright was not as interested in creating gardens or landscapes as he was in integrating the natural environment with the design of his houses. Certainly, he was not interested in making his houses part of a garden."[21]

For Rose, Wright's disinterest in designing the landscape as a place for people to inhabit was a conceptual shortcoming, a way of thinking that was insufficient to address the needs and sensibilities of modern Americans for whom the landscape was also a place for living. This insufficiency was most apparent when Wright built on small, already disturbed or otherwise undistinguished suburban tracts, instead of on landscapes with obvious natural advantages. In such mundane settings, his houses were revealed as unusual if beautiful objects, typically adorned by the same decorative foundation plantings and useless lawns that characterized the rest of the degraded suburban environment.

Rudolph Schindler (who had worked for Wright) first

fully explored the possibilities of abstract, free space and the open plan in a small residential site he designed for himself, his wife, and another couple in West Hollywood, California. Completed in 1922 (seven years before Mies van der Rohe's Barcelona Pavilion), the remarkable Schindler House has been described as "the first modern house to be built in the world."[22] Perhaps it was, but here Schindler did something greater than design a modern house: he created an orthogonal open plan for inhabitable space throughout an entire site. The Schindler House is really a continuum of open space uniting indoors and outdoors, using concrete walls along with hedges, slab floors along with lawn, and wood-framed ceilings along with sky as its edges. If the Schindler House was not actually the first modern house in the world, it was the first modern "house-and-garden," providing abstract but useful designed space for living throughout the site. On his small property in West Hollywood, Schindler exhibited the kind of spatial integration Rose would demand from the Bauhaus architects with whom he became intimately familiar at Harvard fifteen years later. Although Rose never wrote about the Schindler House, the spatial similarities between it and Rose's initial design for his own home are unmistakable (figs. 7a, 7b).

In the design world of the 1920s and 1930s, everyone knew about Frank Lloyd Wright, but in 1932 neither Wright nor Schindler was included in *The International Style,* an influential book prepared by Henry-Russell Hitchcock and Philip Johnson in tandem with the New York Museum of Modern Art's *Modern Architecture: International Exhibition.* Hitchcock and Johnson identified three principles as defining the new style: the expression of volume rather than mass, the emphasis on balance rather than preconceived symmetry, and the expulsion of applied ornament. While Wright,

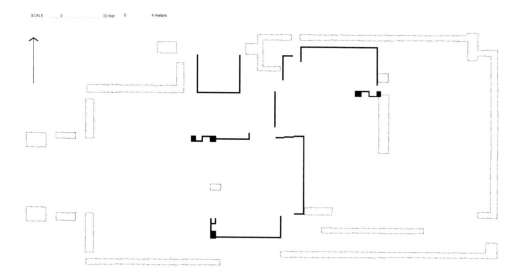

Fig. 7a. Schindler House diagram showing architectural walls and hedges. Drawn by Wenjie Liu and Xiaoxia Wang based on a plan from Kathryn Smith's *Schindler House* (Hennessey & Ingalls, 2010), 35. Courtesy JRC.

a proponent of craftsmanship and the relevance of particular sites, declined to be included in the book, the spatial ideal represented by his open plan was thoroughly embraced.

Like Wright, the pioneering European architect Le Corbusier described architecture metaphorically. However, instead of a building being rooted in its site like a tree, to Le Corbusier a building was a "machine for living," independent of or even in contrast to the landscape around it. Of Le Corbusier's approach, Rose commented, "His landscapes are passive and pastoral, and the structures are dramatically in *conflict* with their environment, forming a kind of yin-yang relation between solid and void."[23] Like Wright, Le Corbusier explored space that was open and free, rather than enclosed and discrete. As Le Corbusier himself wrote, "To put it in a nutshell: we must have plenty of room in order

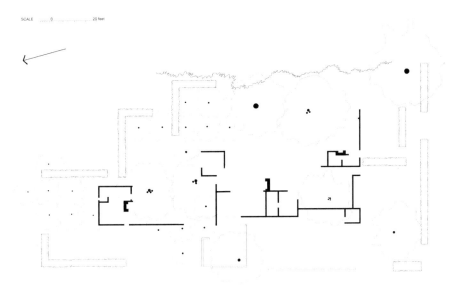

Fig. 7b. Rose house diagram showing walls, hedges, and existing and proposed trees. Drawn by Wenjie Liu and Xiaoxia Wang. Courtesy JRC.

to live in full daylight, so that the 'animal' in us won't feel cooped up, so that it can move about, have space around it and in front of it."[24] While Wright's building forms were integrally tied to their sites and Le Corbusier's were set dramatically against them, both architects embraced the romantic construct of open architectural space as a metaphor for the wild, "natural" space they imagined the landscape to be. Much to Rose's disapproval, neither architect directly engaged the landscape itself as a place for modern living.

The work of Schindler's colleague Richard Neutra was included in the MoMA exhibition and book. Although Neutra's designs extended architectural space into the landscape through glass walls, Rose did not see this approach as an expression of a modern sensibility about the landscape. In Neutra he observed a lazy romanticism in the treatment of the site: "With a brilliant mind, tenacious and undeviating as a bear trap, as far as buildings were concerned, Neutra could relax utterly as a kind of antidote when it came to his gardens. While the qualities of both house and garden were severely pointed up by contrast, neither arrived at even the back door of nature; they were pictorial and romantic in the extreme."[25]

Among the European luminaries included as representatives of the International Style were Mies van der Rohe, whose famous 1929 Barcelona Pavilion distilled abstract modern space, and Walter Gropius, the founder of the Bauhaus and first head of Harvard's Graduate School of Design.[26] They were also among those architects who would alternately inspire and infuriate Rose when he came into contact with them just a few years later at Harvard.

For the most part, landscape architecture contributed little to the conversation in the first third of the twentieth century. The 1925 *Exposition Internationale des Arts Décoratifs et Industriels Modernes* in Paris refuted International Style architects' vision of the landscape as merely a "natural" foil to modern architecture, but in place of that vision the exposition posited landscape designs that celebrated modern form as only two-dimensional ground patterns or as three-dimensional objects set in outdoor frames, treating landscape elements as something to look at in a painterly or sculptural way and failing to address the subject of modern "volumetric space" in landscape terms. Of the Armenian architect Gabriel Guevrekian's Garden of Water and Light (included in the Paris exhibition) and his later, similar garden at the Villa Noailles, the landscape historian Catherine Howett has written, "They are . . . rigorously self-referential and objectified; the materials of the landscape—water, plants, and such architectural elements as the walls and raised beds—are treated as the material for art-making in the way that the inert materials of any art or craft are transformed into an art object. The design places more emphasis on dazzling visual effects of color, light, and perspective than on the kinesthetic experience of plastic and fluid, volumetric space that was an obsessive concern of the early modernist architects"[27] (fig. 8).

In its failure to engage the concept of "fluid, volumetric space"—an issue that would become the obsession of Rose, Kiley, and Eckbo—Guevrekian's garden was typical of landscape works in the Paris exposition, in which André and Paul Vera and Robert Mallet-Stevens were also represented. Rose, writing years later, commented on the incipient signs of landscape modernism in their garden designs, condemning their expressions as superficial and noting that "although appearances had changed, gardens retained a strict symmetry and a static, highly formal, non-functioning, artistic self-consciousness." In an apparent dismissal of their work, he con-

Fig. 8. Gabriel Guevrekian's Garden of Water and Light at the Exposition Internationale des Arts Décoratifs et Industriels Modernes, Paris, 1925.

tinued: "They simplified. They did 'futuristic gardens.' They got rid of ornament. They relinquished grandeur. But when they were all finished, they had another expression of the bind that held them rather than a primal look into the void." Still, Rose allowed that "strangely, even within this limited framework the most conservative of these designers was moving in a direction that was unthinkable to men in a similar position in the design world of the United States at that time."[28]

It was not unthinkable to Fletcher Steele, however, who visited the exposition gardens and was more enthusiastic than Rose about their introduction of new forms (such as zigzags), metaphors (for example, concrete trees), and materials (e.g., mirrors), even if their focus on almost surreal patterns and objects failed to engage a conception of modern volumetric landscape space. In an important article published in *Landscape Architecture* magazine in 1930, Steele extolled the virtues of these projects, drawing analogies between landscape design and other contemporary arts. Steele returned to the necessity of addressing space, however, and in a subsequent article prophesied "that successful space composition will be the next serious preoccupation of landscape architects."[29] Although it could be argued that landscape architects had always attempted to compose space, Rose joined Steele in the belief that the profession had forgotten this. Certainly, the zeal with which Rose, Kiley, and Eckbo would, for the first time, promote the nature of open and continuous space in the landscape was unprecedented.

As Wright championed an indigenous architecture in the Midwest, the landscape architect Jens Jensen, working in that region (sometimes with Wright), introduced his representation of the indigenous prairie, using native trees, shrubs, and grasses. Although his design sense was very much rooted in the nineteenth-century English romantic tradition, Jensen contributed to the mental atmosphere an appreciation for the vernacular landscape and a contemporary expression of the "spirit of place" fundamental to landscape architecture.

Perhaps the single strongest bridge between the Beaux-Arts tradition and the modern revolution in landscape architecture can be seen in the work of Thomas Church (fig. 9). Church's gardens, rooted in the California landscape where he worked, adapted some of the new forms of modern art and European modernist landscapes (zigzags and biomorphic curves), but with a refined spatial sensibility. While Rose expresses his appreciation for Church's work in an early *California Arts and Architecture* article, he later somewhat dismisses Church as "transitional," commenting that Church's "work had a popular appeal that was immediate, nouveau, but with a charm and grace that made it thoroughly acceptable. The breakthrough, however, was not complete; it retained a basic underlying adherence to principles of the old [Beaux-Arts] school while having abundant surface characteristics of the new."[30]

By the mid-1930s the subject of modern landscape architecture, as defined by the exploration of open and continuous landscape space designed to support the outdoor needs of modern people, was waiting to be examined. As Dan Kiley would later ebulliently remark, "It's space and spatial mystery! That's the thing that makes something modern, not a zigzag or a this or a that. 'Modern' is our *present* understanding of space. Nature has nothing to do with 'naturalistic.' It has to do with spatial continuity and spatial mystery. Jim and I, and Garrett too, were always excited about these things, and that is what kept us going."[31]

When Rose landed at Harvard in 1936, his larger world had already been engaged and a sense of infinite possibilities encouraged his inherently rebellious spirit. Despite hav-

Fig. 9. Thomas Church's Sullivan garden, San Francisco, 1935. Courtesy Thomas D. Church Collection, Environmental Design Archives, University of California, Berkeley.

ing lived in relative poverty, Rose was already thoroughly immersed in the new ideas of his times, which provided him with a strong and "fresh view" that soon collided with the uneasy landscape architecture establishment at Harvard. He eloquently characterized the cultural moment in a 1940 essay in *California Arts and Architecture*:

> We have begun the expression of a new age which has all the dignity and some of the greatness of ancient Greek, Medieval, and Renaissance art. It is, nevertheless, based on a different social order and a different source of inspiration. It must therefore be judged by different standards. When thinking and living become completely unified with the process, it will be an indigenous expression of our times with fair opportunity of surpassing any of the previous periods in stature and quality. We must first know and live within our own civilization, rather than beam at it intelligently, like the faces in a cozy painting. We must get rid of the almost unconscious snobbishness which makes us imagine we are getting "culture" at the opera while completely blind to the inventive miracles of the amusement park and the department store. When we look at things again, with a fresh view rather than that of an art catalogue, we will know instinctively when to laugh and when not to laugh at Picasso, and how to build our gardens.[32]

Modern Landscape Space

By the time Rose entered Harvard as a "special student," he had already gone around or through obstacles encountered in other schools. He never graduated from DeWitt Clinton High School, having refused to take required courses that he considered irrelevant, but in 1931 he somehow managed to enroll at Cornell, where he studied agriculture. While there, he also took courses in architecture, literature, and the theater, including a playwriting class, and acted in university productions of contemporary plays whenever he could. When he transferred into Harvard's Graduate School of Design, he met Garrett Eckbo and Dan Kiley. As Eckbo recalled,

> In the fall of 1936 I went east to Harvard GSD on a scholarship. Jim and I met, and were almost instant friends. We roomed together in Cambridge, encountered modern architecture in Gropius and Breuer, were fascinated by modernism (the profession had never heard of anything so outlandish), jousted with the faculty and most of the other students (except Dan Kiley, who supported us), developed our own concepts of modern design, and in general had a ball.[33]

Characteristically, Rose recalls the scene at Harvard more theatrically in *Modern American Gardens—Designed by James Rose* (which he wrote surreptitiously under the pseudonym Marc Snow). One senses Rose's delight in referring to himself in the third person while describing what went on within the landscape program:

> The academic smoulder over abstract principles of design flamed into an open student revolt. The chief protagonists, Garrett Eckbo, Daniel Kiley, and James Rose, on the student side of the drama, seem to have

been alternately outraged by the academic restrictions of the Mayflower hierarchy and exultant in having such a beautifully classic adversary against whom to do battle. They experimented secretly, unbeknownst to the landscape faculty, on designs in the forbidden area of the modern idiom. These clandestine experiments were held in Cambridge rooming houses and in the basement of Robinson Hall, somewhat in the manner of early medical students dissecting corpses in secret to gain a firsthand knowledge of anatomy. Like the school teacher with eyes in the back of her head, Harvard, on the faculty side of the drama, knew perfectly well what was going on and was not in the least amused.[34]

Design at Harvard was already in a state of transition when Rose, Kiley, and Eckbo arrived.[35] In the fall of 1936 Joseph Hudnut had just established the Graduate School of Design, unifying landscape architecture, architecture, and city planning. A host of modern, mostly European architectural luminaries, including Walter Gropius, Josef Albers, Marcel Breuer, and Sigfried Giedeon, was soon to arrive, with the English landscape architect Christopher Tunnard to follow.[36] All of this was much to the dismay of the landscape faculty, which adhered stubbornly to an approach Rose described as "Beaux-Arts neoclassical French and Italian style." To the younger Rose, Kiley, and Eckbo, who came to Harvard from modest financial backgrounds, in the midst of a lingering economic depression—and during a time of global democratization and radically new scientific discoveries about, and artistic expressions of, time, space, and consciousness—designing Beaux-Arts style estates for wealthy patrons on Long Island was simply irrelevant. Nor could such a distantly conceived approach as the Beaux-Arts be adapted, as its contemporary apologists suggested, to the needs and sensibilities of people living in the radically different times of the 1930s. As Rose quipped years later, "Christ, even if you could find a site just like the Villa D'Este, where were you going to find Mr. D'Este?"[37]

Harvard, indeed, was not amused by Rose's antics. From the beginning of his enrollment his days were numbered, and he was summarily dropped from the landscape school after the 1937 spring semester. As he told the story, "The assignment was posted on the board, and at the bottom it read, 'Anyone attempting one of those 'modernistic' solutions will receive an 'X.' Well, I did a 'modernistic' solution, got an 'X,' did more 'modernistic' solutions, got more 'Xs,' and eventually they 'X'-pelled me. I took my 'Xs' to *Pencil Points* magazine, and they gave me a two-year contract!"[38] Rose's subsequent *Pencil Points* articles, based on those Xs and on the experiments he conducted in that Cambridge rooming house where he lived with Garrett Eckbo, were significant, even seminal, in establishing the history and theory of the art of modern landscape design. Those writings signaled the beginning of an evolving personal inquiry into the art of designing contemporary landscape space that would continue throughout his life.

In his *Pencil Points* articles Rose generally condemns the landscape establishment for its failure to recognize and respond to the new mental atmosphere of the times with new forms and approaches to the landscape. To Rose, the profession had lost its way as a contemporary spatial art by relying on irrelevant, predetermined design formulas and by employing a two-dimensional, pictorial mode of graphic representation that limited the exploration of a new, freer conception of landscape space attuned to the continually changing needs of modern people.

In "Freedom in the Garden" (October 1938), Rose vehemently counters arguments proffered by proponents of the Beaux-Arts status quo against the idea of a new approach to modern landscape design (fig. 10). He draws on the manifold expressions of modern space, time, and consciousness in dance, theater, poetry, painting, sculpture, music, and architecture to illustrate the pervasiveness and character of a radically changed sensibility. Noting that the same nine notes of music were used by both Bach and Stravinsky and that the unchanged human body was used in the Greek chorus as well as by the Ballet Russe, he excoriates the arrière-garde position that, since the materials used to make space in the landscape have not changed, there is no need for or possibility of a contemporary landscape expression. With characteristic rhetorical flourish, Rose concludes, "We have found our final resting place. Our grave is on axis in a Beaux-Arts cemetery. A monument terminates the vista, and if you approach with reverence, you can see the bromitaph authority has placed there: 'A tree is a tree, and always will be a tree; therefore we can have no modern landscape design.'"[39]

Having summarily dismissed objections to the idea of modern landscape design, Rose considers what a modern landscape spatial conception might be. To the comparisons between modern paintings, constructions, and architectural drawings established by Alfred H. Barr Jr. in his Museum of Modern Art exhibition and catalog *Cubism and Abstract Art* (1936), and an image of Naum Gabo's sculpture *Construction Spherique* reproduced from Carola Giedion-Welcker's *Modern Plastic Art* (1937), Rose adds the landscape drawings and models for which he was expelled from Harvard. Spatial relationships are clear and undeniable. It is important to note, however, that in cataloging his experiments in landscape design with these other expressions of modern art, Rose is

FREEDOM IN
THE GARDEN

A CONTEMPORARY APPROACH IN LANDSCAPE DESIGN

BY JAMES C. ROSE

Landscape design falls somewhere between architecture and sculpture. Relieved of most structural and use requirements in the architectural sense, it is less purely æsthetic than sculpture because of circulation requirements. In reality, it is outdoor sculpture, not to be looked at as an object, but designed to surround us in a pleasant sense of space relations. It differs from both architecture and sculpture in several important respects:

1. Materials, for the most part, are living and growing.

2. Horizontal dimension is usually much greater in relation to the vertical, a fact that increases the difficulty in getting a sense of volume and third dimension.

3. Scale, determined by the sky and surrounding country, is necessarily larger.

4. A sense of form is more difficult to achieve because of the looseness and instability

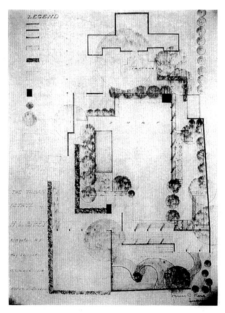

Aesthetic division of space imparts distinction to the garden plan, at left, by the author, who seeks to preserve in materials abstract relations such as those expressed in Picasso's "Figure," below, reproduced from "Cubism and Abstract Art" by courtesy of the Museum of Modern Art, New York City

639

Fig. 10. "Freedom in the Garden," *Pencil Points* (October 1938).

not suggesting that landscape architecture mimic their *forms;* his models were not made to respond to these artworks, nor is landscape design the same as painting, sculpture, or architecture. By pointing out the differences between landscape design and other arts and architecture in scale, use, and materials, as well as its uniquely impermanent, loose, and changing nature, Rose is demonstrating that his early landscape experiments both share an artistic sensibility with other modern arts and are distinct from them.

Rose's early experiments in modern landscape space were abstractly related, asymmetrical, complex, open yet volumetric, and continuous though interrupted. They were to be experienced kinesthetically from within (unlike painting and sculpture), simultaneously imprinting an infinite number of "views" or, more accurately, "perceptions" on the mind as one moved through them.[40] Constantly changing with one's motion and with the changes in time, these almost kaleidoscopic experiences should, Rose argued, express their fundamental materials of earth, rock, water, plants, and any new synthetic materials together, honestly and directly, arriving at a "space-form" that was an organic response to them, to their technologies, and to contemporary people's distinctive landscape uses, problems, and sensibilities. As Rose summarizes in "Articulate Form in Landscape Design" (1939), "When we permit our minds to grasp the new conception of space, and learn to use materials for their own quality, we will develop an organic style. When we consider people and circulation first, instead of clinging to the imitation of classic ornament, we will develop an animated landscape expressive of contemporary life; and catch words like *symmetry, axis,* and *informal* will be known for their true significance . . . practically nothing."[41]

In so arguing for a modern expression of landscape space,

Rose's condemnation of the Beaux-Arts system as it was presented by his instructors at Harvard is really a more nuanced argument against a method of teaching and representing landscape space that he understood as formulaic (predetermined), two-dimensional, and pictorial rather than spontaneous, kinesthetic, and phenomenal. Such a method might have worked in the past, but, as Rose put it, in the 1930s, it was "fundamentally wrong to begin with axes or shapes in plan; ground forms evolve from a division of space."[42] In "Plants Dictate Garden Forms," responding to an article in *Landscape Architecture Quarterly* that called for the adaptation of European precedents for "greater utility and ornament" rather than the development of new spatial conceptions, Rose defiantly elaborates on his spatial theory: "The war cry is often heard that we must combine use and beauty; but by this is meant that we should develop a ground pattern of segregated, geometric areas strung along an axis in Beaux-Arts relationship and separated by 'embellishments' which compose a picture for the terminal point of each area. Something to look at!" He expounds that "we cannot live in pictures, and therefore a landscape designed as a series of pictures robs us of the opportunity to use that area for animated living."[43]

Rose's aesthetic argument, then, is less against symmetry, and the apparently inevitable axis and segregated room organization that result from applying the Beaux-Arts teaching method, than against any design method that begins with a formal premise. In "Articulate Form in Landscape Design," Rose asserts that "when we begin with any preconceived notion of form . . . we eliminate the possibility of developing a form which will articulate and express the activity to occur." He points out that an axis or symmetry could be the product of an organic contemporary approach but stresses that "*form is a result* and not a pre-determined element of the problem."[44] Nor is Rose's frustration with applying the Beaux-Arts system to contemporary landscape spatial design a failure to recognize that such landscapes *are* spatial. Rather, he is asserting that dynamic modern landscape space, as he and his colleagues understand it, cannot be created by pre-determined formulas, nor can it be explored and expressed by a method of working in which selected, fixed points from which to draw perspectival images at the ends of vistas are established in a two-dimensional plan.

To address the need for a more dynamic, fluid spatial conception, Rose promoted designing with landscape models, a method he would later use (then abandon) in his professional practice. Unlike what he called "paper" design, which limited spatial possibilities, working in three-dimensional models offered the opportunity to explore more complex and open space from infinite points of view, as he argues in "Landscape Models":

> In the model, we consider all problems at once and from all points of view: ground modeling, circulation, use, the forms of materials, and immaterial space. Rather than façades, pictures, and plan areas, we deal with time and space in relation to people and material—the perspective experience of people moving in free space interrupted by landscape materials to surround the individual at all times and in all locations with a variety and balance of forms, and direct his experience and circulation.[45]

The three-dimensional model freed designers from the restraints inherent in representing the infinite possibilities of landscape space in a two-dimensional medium. In *Modern American Gardens* Rose reflects on his model-making experience, observing that "as a discipline, it was invaluable. Through this method he [Rose] developed a high sensitivity to spatial balance."[46] But despite such advantages, in "Landscape Models" Rose acknowledges the limitations of modeling landscape space, noting that "the scale model is the medium nearest to actuality—a diagram of forms in relation to the space which surrounds them and the people who use the space—but it can never hope to reproduce the subtleties of nature or the seasonal variations of the actual landscape."[47]

After a period of using models to represent actual landscapes in his professional practice, Rose was confronted by the limitations of the medium that he had foreseen in his early articles, and so he began to design and build directly and spontaneously on-site. In an interesting challenge of Rose's approach, A. E. Bye, in a review of *Modern American Gardens* published in *Landscape Architecture* magazine, argued that "the landscape architect must be responsible to the client and is not free to proceed without a carefully constructed plan." After critiquing all angular modern garden forms in general, Bye pointed out that spontaneity in music and the visual arts was nothing new but argued that it was inappropriate in landscape design, "for the garden is to be enjoyed for years and cannot be dismissed as easily as a canvas or an afternoon of music." Bye also asserted that Rose's use of models, as well as the quality evident in Rose's "constructed ideas," suggested that his gardens were not as spontaneous as Marc Snow had dramatized.[48]

If a bit peevish, Bye's critique was not completely without merit. Still, while even Rose's most mature designs are not entirely free of some degree of forethought and preconception, unlike Bye and perhaps Thomas Church before him, Rose was evolving a method in which the site, rather than the client, was supreme—a method in which the process of making the work was as important as the "finished" product. For Rose, making gardens became more of an ephemeral and ethereal art than a profession, to be practiced in situ while working directly with one's materials, like sculpture or most any other art form. "Paper" design, he explains through Marc Snow,

> the technique of communicating a garden on the two-dimensional surface of a sheet of paper . . . is standard procedure in most schools and offices, eminently suited to the filing and classification of drawings. But . . . , if not certain death to the making of a garden, it is at least so far removed from what a garden is that it is "like a doctor trying to explain over the telephone how to perform an appendectomy when he isn't even sure that the patient has appendicitis." For Rose, the garden experience is a sculptural one, direct, and in at least the three dimensions of length, width, and height within space and time. This can be accomplished only by working directly with and in them.[49]

The vitality of his approach is evident in the gardens themselves and should be instructive to designers, even if its full embrace may be unsuitable to the profession.

Rose's early *Pencil Points* critique extended beyond the arrière-garde of landscape architecture to encompass the avant-garde of modern architecture, especially the Bauhaus architects who came to dominate Harvard in the 1930s. In "Integration," he writes:

> Landscape design exists in an isolated world of never-changing aestheticism. . . . Architects have sinned

more progressively. They have built a kind of scenic railway in design where anyone may get a thrill who takes the ride, but after a few nostalgic moments, the passenger is delivered to precisely the point where he got on, and whence he continues the haphazardry of his existence. With a few notable exceptions, architects have made no attempt to express any human experience outside the walls of a building. Houses are now, more than ever, designed as a special entity, wrapped in a package, and delivered to the public. No matter how closely they may resemble a "machine for living," they are still an objet d'art, and as such, may provide a momentary thrill and eventually become interesting to collectors, but at present, they have little relation to the rest of the world in which living also occurs.

Isn't it a little inconsistent, and perhaps unfair, to expect a Twentieth Century individual to step out of a stream-lined automobile, and then flounder through a Rousseauian wilderness until he reaches a "machine for living"? We cannot confine living, which is a process, to little segregated compartments that end at the edge of the nearest terrace where we are again asked to adjust ourselves to what, in its highest form, becomes an Eighteenth Century landscape painting.[50]

In *Modern American Gardens,* Rose ruminates on the architectural climate at Harvard, writing that, "while the presence of Gropius and the others was an encouragement, the architectural school became dominated by the Bauhaus view which was certainly an improvement, but didn't exactly fit the indigenous American scene. For Rose it was 'pure,' and perhaps basic enough for the environment that produced it, but it was essentially an importation and had a sterility which lacked what he calls the 'cosmic *joie.*' "[51] The Bauhaus was an improvement chiefly because of its concern for abstract modern space, but in its austere universal aspirations, it failed to recognize the important role of context and of the landscape, much less the need to design that landscape for people.

Although Rose was profoundly critical of contemporary landscape architecture for its failure to recognize and respond to the realities of twentieth-century American life, and of contemporary architecture for its failure to recognize that the landscape needed to be designed for modern living, he saw a useful analogue to modern landscape architecture in some modern sculpture. In "Freedom in the Garden," he observes that "the constructivists probably have the most to offer landscape design because their work deals with space relations in volume. The sense of transparency, and of visibility broken by a succession of planes, as found in their constructions, if translated into terms of outdoor material, would be an approach sufficient in itself to free us from the limitations imposed by the axial system."[52] The sculptural analogue to landscape was perhaps most useful to Rose; he referred to it again and again throughout his life. For example, in *Creative Gardens* he writes of finding it helpful to think of the garden as sculpture—"not sculpture in the ordinary sense of an object to be viewed. But sculpture that is large enough and perforated enough to walk through. And open enough to present no barrier to movement, and broken enough to guide the experience, which is essentially a communion with the sky."[53]

Rose's theoretical and polemical exploration of modern landscape space in the 1930s and early 1940s was grounded in the new mental atmosphere of his times and in the nature of landscape design as a distinct art form. He was asked to return to Harvard, and he did, though he never graduated. Things were happening there, but he soon became restless, wanting to get on with his career as a practicing landscape architect. He would have to surmount other significant obstacles along his zigzag path, however, before he could focus on building that career.

Pacific Islands Interlude

At the end of the 1930s, opportunities for a young modern landscape architect were limited in the northeastern United States. In 1940 Rose left Harvard and the East Coast on a road trip with Christopher Tunnard, stopping at Black Mountain College in North Carolina to visit with Josef Albers before continuing through the South and Southwest to California, making professional contacts along the way. After arriving in Los Angeles, Rose stayed in a basement apartment in Frank Lloyd Wright's Freeman house, joined Butler Davenport's Free Theater, and became more optimistic about the possibilities for a practice on the West Coast. This optimism is readily apparent in a letter to his mother written shortly after he got to Los Angeles:

> We [Rose and Tunnard] are going up to San Francisco to see Garrett [Eckbo] sometime next week and then back here. I am going to get a little studio the first of April, and try to make a go of things. . . . I am giving a lecture at the Bel Aire garden club sometime in April ($25), and meeting the President Monday. They have all the money in the world, I guess, and they want me to tell them what is wrong

with their development. There seems to be plenty of opportunity for doing something out here, but that is probably too good to be true. I am talking to the general public on the public library series of lectures April 25, covering the material in the Architectural Record. Also a talk to student groups and the Civic Beautification Club in April. My friends tell me this is just the beginning, but we shall see. . . . Please be sure to send all my things as I will need everything. It is all a long chance, but I think it will work—certainly better than anything in the east.[54]

Unfortunately, it *was* all too good to be true. Rose did begin lecturing and writing for *California Arts and Architecture,* and he made his first gardens in 1940 and early 1941, but it was still hard "to make a go of things" since the military needs of the prewar economy had yet to ripple into a full recovery from the Great Depression.[55] After only a little more than a year in California, Rose returned to the East Coast, where he took a job (his only professional office job) with the Czech-born architect Antonin Raymond; Raymond had recently established a practice in New Hope, Pennsylvania, only one hundred or so miles downriver from Rose's family home in Matamoras. In New Hope, Raymond complemented his New York City office of Tuttle, Seelye, Place and Raymond with a practice based more on Wright's model for Taliesin, enabling him to more fully explore his interest in fusing modern architecture with Japanese craftsmanship.[56] Like Tunnard, Raymond would prove to be a good friend and mentor to Rose. According to Rose's literary alter ego, Marc Snow, Raymond "first came in contact with Rose through Rose's early articles and garden designs which appeared in *Pencil Points.* When the situation of war work arose, he was able to see the potential of the peculiar ability behind these designs for large-scale planning."[57] Working for Raymond in the lead-up to the United States' entry into World War II, Rose designed the staging area at Camp Kilmer, New Jersey. As Snow describes it:

> From gardens to anti-aircraft regiments is not the smallest jump imaginable—that is, if you don't know what scale is—and Rose apparently did. No aesthetics are required for anti-aircraft regiments, just fool-proof schematic organization that works like a machine and will not break down under the stress and pressure of speed, incompetence, personal ambitions, lack of know-how, and all the other weaknesses that hastily organized large-scale projects are heir to.[58]

In ninety days Camp Kilmer was ready for troops, and it would not be long before Rose himself would enlist in the navy and experience firsthand those defects of people and large-scale organizations so cynically described in *Modern American Gardens*. Armed with a pack of Kools, the works of Plato (between the pages of which he pressed flowers), and a deck of cards, Rose was skeptical of the war from the outset. Artistic, gifted, and gay, his acute sense of being different as well as his longing to be understood and accepted on his terms, were already firmly embedded as he anticipated his wartime experience. From basic training at his barracks in Williamsburg, Virginia, in the first of what would be hundreds of revealing, intimate biweekly letters to his adoring mother (who saved them all), Rose wistfully writes,

> I won't be fighting for all the little people as the radio says. My world is too big for that. I won't be fight-

ing for anything. I'll just be there, like the sunrise or snow in April. . . . Snow in April is a little out of place but so are people like me with so much more and so much less than our little world understands. But have you ever thought what a beautiful sound April has? You should have been born in April. It's the sound of "April" I'll be fighting for. What more can I say.[59]

During his time in the service, with its red-tape ineffi-ciencies and injustices and its intimate exposure of human greed and jealousy under stress, Rose became increasingly disillusioned, alienated, and embittered. As he moved from basic training to the Pacific front, his efforts to express his creativity became bogged down in the military's demand for conformity. He lost his privacy, and he daily confronted what he saw as the mounting hypocrisies of the war. In his letters home he refers to himself and his fellow sailors as "inmates," but he explains that he has found escape through his imagination, withdrawing to what he calls a "little island in the mind." Writing to his mother while stationed in the Mariana Islands, after he has outlined a list of what he sees as absurd military activities performed by others, he reflects on an isolation that is only partly self-imposed:

I've been quite happy here, as things go, pursuing my own plans. It makes me serene and peaceful and confident because I know that there is a whole world of people and things I like or that please. It's not easy to get there. It requires some basic decisions and many privations that are quite as real and diffi-cult as any vows of the church. But I don't mean to imply anything heroic or sacrificial. There is little of that. It's more a question of values, and the choice is not entirely with one's self. I suppose where you find yourself in the scale of things is simply the result of all the pressures acting upon you and to which you react until you find an equilibrium. Well, that's what I've found. And if I've found it here I can find it anywhere in the world. You can probably guess the kind of confidence just the knowledge of that equilibrium gives you. And to be quite certain of your own choice as well as aware of and grateful for the "gift" for which you can assume no credit are things that make all the gold in the service seem like a well licked platter as compared with a good old fashioned Irish stew.

It's the nearest thing I've ever known to peace and fulfillment. It's like a little island in the mind that has no defenses and is yet perfectly secure against attack. The petty world intrudes itself at times like planes flying overhead and so far away you can scarcely hear the motors. You can't help but wonder who pilots these things and what it's like out there and where they're all going, anyway.

From my island, the rest of the world is like the mad rush to the beach on an August Sunday. . . . You can easily see that such "world shaking" things as fear and greed and envy and petty ambitions have no place on this island of mine. Everything is free and nothing can be taken from you. And as long as I stay there, I am invulnerable.[60]

At the beginning of his navy service Rose had hoped to be able to offer more of himself, but, as had been the case his whole life, he was frustrated and disillusioned by what he saw as the injustice and hypocrisy of authority and its demand for conformity. As his wartime service unfolded Rose made every effort to relieve himself of military chores, finding peace and confidence in a private creative world of reading, writing in his "Crazy Book," sketching, painting, and model making. To facilitate the last of these activities, he began scavenging for materials, looking for things that, like him, had been discarded or overlooked. Motivated by the creative force within him, Rose used his imagination to see what others did not; his scavenging technique, as he describes it in a letter to his mother, was simple: "I just wait. Invariably the things I'm most interested in are left because no one sees the same use for them that I do. . . . They cannot see the value of things unless purely monetary."[61]

Such scavenging would provide Rose with the raw materials for constructing a model of a postwar dream home that he designed for himself, his mother, and his sister Jean (fig. 11). He initially conceived the home being built along the Delaware River at his family's property in Matamoras, Pennsylvania, and later along a meandering stream in Connecticut. (It ultimately was constructed in 1952–1953 in suburban Ridgewood, New Jersey, on a tiny, leftover, unvalued scrap of land beside the Ho-Ho-Kus Brook.) In another letter home to his mother, Rose details how he reused the materials he scavenged:

> You will be amazed at the things in my model. It's built on a piece of stolen plywood cut to its present shape with the battalion saws and nailed together with "borrowed" nails. I bribed one of the mess cooks for some galley flour which, with the brown paper wrapping off your first package, made some excellent paper mache for modeling the river bank. The armature for the paper mache is wire screening "borrowed" while

Fig. 11. Rose holding a model of his dream home, 1944. Courtesy JRC.

the mess hall was under construction. The tacks that fasten it to the plywood were "procured" from the tent area while the tents were being screened. Each day I come home from the field ladened in pockets and hands with an odd assortment of [illegible] I've collected in the field. (I'm just a scavenger at heart, I guess. I remind myself of Uncle Fred collecting tin cans and poles to make an apple picker.) . . . I also have redwood strips made from surveying stakes, which I use for the roof. The window glass will be cut from thin celluloid lenses from Japanese gas masks which I found today in a wild mosquito infested bivouac near where we work. The hedges are made from clothes stops. I can't describe the intricacies of making all these things, but to give you an idea, I found some insulated wire which is made up of seven strands. Three of these are soft lead and four are stiff and springy like piano wire, but smaller. I take the lead wire and wind it around the clothes stops at approximately half-inch intervals and then cut just below the wire. This holds the cord together at the bottom and allows it to fray at the top. When painted and cemented to the model it looks a lot like shrubbery.[62]

As George Skrubb, a friend Rose made during the war, recalled, "In Rose's hands, scraps became symbols of something else; with them, he was inventing a design language of his own—a puzzling thought, on the hills of Okinawa."[63] Indeed, to satisfy his obsessive frugality, as well as for expressive reasons, Rose continued to reuse unvalued scraps in the gardens he made after the war, a tendency that would become an integral and distinctive part of his work.

Rose's imagination counterpoised his agony at being trapped in the Mariana Islands and then on Okinawa during the war, but he could not always live on his private "island in the mind." As time passed, his cynicism and frustration with authority, injustice, meaningless tasks, and the irrational demands of others often boiled over. In a letter to his mother written in April 1945, his anger and frustration are evident:

I'm finished with chores and don't expect to do any, except the official ones until I get out of the service and then I don't expect to do any at all—ever again. I'm going to retire immediately and do nothing except the things I like to do. . . . As of the day I get out I become 100% unsocial. I don't want any of the "benefits" except those with no strings attached and none of the obligations even if it's more trouble to avoid them.[64]

Mercifully for Rose, the conclusion of the war was nearing, and he would soon resume his nascent career, but the war's impact on him, as revealed in his letters to his mother, was enormous. On August 6 and 9, 1945, Hiroshima and Nagasaki were atomic bombed. By August 11, the war had effectively ended—and, along with it, what little remained of Rose's idealistic faith in the modern world. His navy service on those Pacific islands had cemented his disrespect for authority and sealed his sense of alienation from society, while also empowering his personal imagination and will. Rose's negative response to authority, first in school and then in the military, foreshadowed his future confrontations with those official forces that would mindlessly destroy the natural world in the postwar American suburbs that were already beginning to form somewhere in the distance, beyond the smoke and clouds of the Pacific theater. In a letter to his mother describing the jubilation of the men on the base once word came through the loudspeaker that the war was over, Rose shares his own feelings of disillusionment as he walked back to the barracks:

> For my part, I walked home along the ridge feeling very safe amidst the crazy, random firing of liberated GIs. For it has never been the danger or the physical pain or the thoughts of death that have bothered me.

I minded these only from the instinct of preservation and the thoughts of what you might suffer if I did not. The intolerable part is the stupidity of military procedures, the sub-animal level to which men will sink at the first opportunity, the degrading services they will perform for the prestige of an extra ribbon, the sanctioned corruption of our "gentlemen," the exposure of democracy as a mythical cover for official insolence. I could go on, but you can't make much out of rotten eggs. I don't even know our enemy, but I don't see how they could represent more evil than is already among us.

Rose concludes the letter with a reference to Malcolm's speech in *Macbeth* on hearing of his father's murder: "'My tears are not yet brewed,' but walking home was a beautiful sight—something like the innocent beauty of a young face that you've seen distorted and capable of the ugliest crime. You can never quite believe in it again."[65]

Suburbia Transformed

Rose's need to "make a go of things" (fueled in part by his desire to be sure his mother was provided for), his intense feelings of disillusionment, and his growing awareness of the power of his imagination all contributed to his uniquely practical and artistic career path after the war. In 1946, capitalizing on his prewar publications and contacts, Rose set up an office on the Lower West Side of New York City, where he also resided. During his time in the city, his evolving ideas about landscape space became manifest in numerous experimental built residential landscapes in the emerging postwar suburbs, as well as in other types of projects throughout the United States and in other countries (figs. 12, 13). As the architect Eleanore Pettersen, with whom Rose would later collaborate, described it, Rose's practice quickly evolved into "a big office in New York . . . employing several model makers, with projects all over the place."[66]

Rose began lecturing at Columbia University (an arrangement that lasted for six years) and Cooper Union, and he resumed publishing articles in popular magazines and professional architectural journals, including *Ladies' Home Journal, McCall's, House Beautiful, Architectural Forum,* and *Progressive Architecture.* For Rose, his successful postwar career—combining teaching, writing, and designing—helped strengthen the already important reciprocal relationship between theory and practice, between ideas and space. This was evidenced not only by his distinctive postwar landscapes but also by his penetrating criticism and imaginative prose.

In his first book, *Creative Gardens,* Rose uses over a decade of built work to help him tell a story about his adventures making gardens in the American suburbs.[67] While his commercial publisher (Reinhold) may have been looking for a best-selling coffee-table book, *Creative Gardens* was nothing of the kind.[68] Rose thought of it as an "art book," but it is also a work of literature, a kind of landscape drama satirizing authority and the typical contemporary American conformist attitude represented by 1950s suburbia. As would be the case with all his books, Rose's theatrical presentation was intended to reach the general public, including, of course, any prospective clients who might want to hire him for their projects. Less direct in its presentation than Eckbo's seminal *Landscape for Living* (published eight years earlier), *Creative Gardens* communicates much of its message about modern landscape design through the stories Rose tells of his confrontations

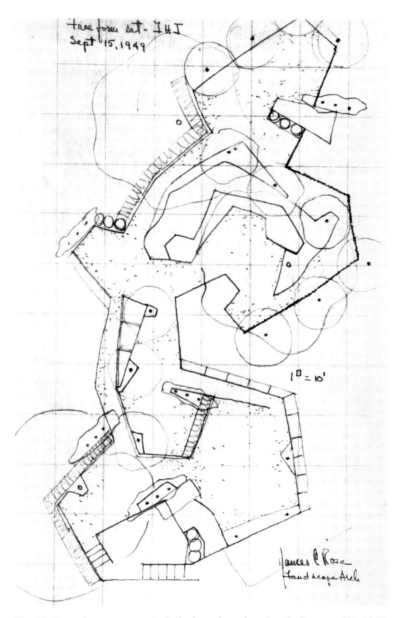

tree form set - IHT
Sept 15, 1949

1" = 10'

James C Rose
Landscape Arch

Fig. 12. Irregular geometry in Seibel garden plan, South Orange, NJ, 1949.
Courtesy JRC.

Fig. 13. Modular garden in Great Neck, NY, 1949. Photograph by Ezra Stoller. © Ezra Stoller/Esto.

with convention. Occasionally quixotic, frequently inspired, Rose slips naturally into an observant and enlightened persona who is as creative with words as he is with plants and fiberglass, using anecdotes and metaphors, along with allusions to literature, film, and theater, to write about the postwar American landscape he was encountering (fig. 14).

In *Creative Gardens,* practical, environmental, and spiritual problems in suburbia spawned by the mindless conformity fomented by authority are exposed and then resolved by a decidedly unconventional landscape architect. The book's antagonists include fraudulent advertising executives, greedy developers, "fascist" planners, self-indulgent architects, robotic building inspectors, and naive clients, all of whom unwittingly conspire to degrade the environment and the quality of life, which of course are inseparable. At center stage, Rose, the maverick protagonist, provides a heroic alternative simply by being rational, open, and alert to his environment. He is acutely critical of the "system," creative and unsentimental about nature, yet unconventionally responsive to natural features and systems in his frankly modern designs, which he describes through photographs, sketches, and axonometric plans.[69]

By interweaving graphic descriptions of his projects with ironic stories of his exploits, Rose provides catharsis for the environmental degradation and banality of suburbia he has exposed. Unburdened by preconception, unfettered

Fig. 14. Rose at home, mid-1950s. Courtesy JRC.

by social convention, undaunted even by law, our clear-headed, imaginative hero insightfully combats the epidemic of suburbia one project at a time; in so doing, he reaches a kind of enlightenment, producing undeniably eloquent passages about the essence of all gardens, along with the gardens themselves: "A garden is an experience. It is not flowers, or plants of any kind. It is not flagstone, brick, grass, or pebbles. It is not a barbeque, or a Fiberglas screen. It is an experience. If it were possible to distill the essence of a garden, I think it would be the sense of being within something while still out of doors. That is the substance of it; for until you have that, you do not have a garden at all"[70] (fig. 15).

If the essence of gardens was spatial and experiential, making them was personal for Rose, providing him with the opportunity, in what for him was an alienating and insane suburbia, to rediscover that private island of equilibrium he had found within the madness of the Pacific. While it is very clear that Rose's foremost purpose in designing any garden was to realize his creative process, it is also clear that he hoped to inspire others through their experience of the spaces he was making. He recognized that the emerging environmental and spiritual problems already evident to him were less a by-product of what people were doing than the result of what they were thinking (or not thinking)—and materialistic, conventional-minded Americans were certainly not thinking creatively about nature or landscape space. By 1958, having informed his own prewar spatial thinking with scores of professional garden-making experiences, Rose had gone beyond an academic conception of landscape space to assert its basic human purpose in an environmentally destructive, commodity-conscious, postwar American landscape. In *Creative Gardens* he explains that "this [spatial thinking] could become nothing more than an academic exercise if it were

Fig. 15. South Orange garden, 1954. Photograph by Lonnie Wasco. Courtesy JRC.

done without further purpose. But there is a further purpose and that is to create a frame of reference which will make our perception of nature more acute. The whole purpose is nothing more than this; and this is an infinity."[71]

While *Creative Gardens* is full of projects that celebrate the outdoor social life of the postwar suburban American family (in part so that Rose could appeal to potential clients), it clearly reveals Rose's real interest in making creative, spiritual, and ecological gardens, which would enable him to dwell in his "private island" of renewal while reuniting desensitized Americans with nature through the design of spatial experiences in gardens. But for Rose, what type of spatial experience could change the way modern Americans perceived themselves and nature in a Western industrialized culture? What would be its materials, forms, and characteristics?

There could be no enlightening spatial experience without what Rose called "stuff," those things that define space and fuse with it to become something new. As foreshadowed in several of his early *Pencil Points* articles, Rose's 1950s suburban garden spaces were defined by an assortment of carefully considered materials, including not only the traditional "natural" materials of garden making (plants, rocks, earth, and water) but also new and surprising (if common) modern materials, such as fiberglass, metals, plastics, and blacktop.[72] Significantly, he sought to integrate already existing site features such as trees and outcroppings, as well as to repurpose, rather than throw out, other materials he found on the sites. As he had done in Okinawa, Rose scavenged his suburban environment for overlooked or discarded things that might serve his creative purposes. No doubt the most significant of the items he recovered was the railroad tie, a symbol of American expansion and the conflicts between industrialization and nature. Rose used railroad ties to make steps and walls for terraces in private suburban gardens as early as 1946.[73] Though he eventually lost some of his enthusiasm for many modern materials, Rose would continue to use railroad ties (and other scavenged materials) throughout his career. Incessantly creative and obsessively frugal, he later even used the scraps of railroad ties that were left over from wall and step making to construct spontaneously conceived benches, lanterns, and other site features (fig. 16).

In 1946 Rose's original and surprising reuse of railroad ties in suburban gardens was a unique and thoroughly modern expression. Since the early twentieth century, other modern artists had used common "found objects" to make reliefs, sculptures, and constructions by removing the objects from their original physical and cultural context, manipulating them

Fig. 16. Terraces made from recycled and unusual materials, Macht house and garden, Baltimore, 1957. Photograph by Ezra Stoller. © Ezra Stoller/Esto.

(though never past the point of recognition), and re-presenting them in a new and surprising context (usually the art gallery). Similarly, Rose discovered railroad ties, removed them from their original context, manipulated them into walls and steps, and re-presented them in postwar suburban gardens. Rose's use of railroad ties, blacktop, scrap metal, and other unexpected materials helped give his garden spaces an edgy and surprising, if not shocking, feeling—not entirely unlike how Marcel Duchamp's *Fountain* had shocked patrons of the fine arts several decades earlier.[74] Through his choice of materials alone, Rose created spaces that reflected new ideas, not just new technologies; this was an aspect that appealed to his sensibility, and one that he hoped his clients might perceive.

Abandoned railroad ties were free for the taking, and Rose could see both the aesthetic and the practical value of using them in his gardens. Working with ties to make walls and steps provided a flexibility that allowed him to design three-dimensionally in situ and to spontaneously change his design as he built. The ties also allowed him to choreograph movement beside, around, and through existing site features and thereby engage what was already on-site as part of his spatial geometry. They supported his development of a distinctive geometry that was inherent in ties as a building material and that was reminiscent of a modern spatial sensibility, as expressed in the abstract cubist paintings he had both cited (and created) before and during World War II. Modular, segmented, and lineal, but not necessarily orthogonal, when assembled into steps and retaining walls railroad ties enabled development of a dynamic, flexible, obtuse-angled, three-dimensional spatial experience that, in combination with the use of existing site features, would become characteristic of Rose's work throughout his career. His use of railroad ties helped him to develop the freer, more open space-form he was seeking, one expressive of his materials, the particular features of his sites, his own abstract formal sensibility, and his perceived need for his modern suburban clients to reconcile with nature. In finding and redeploying the railroad tie in the garden, Rose articulated the "free-wheeling way of looking for form" that his good friend Garrett Eckbo described them both as sharing from the start.[75]

For Rose, solving individual garden problems that shouldn't have been created in the first place was not enough. As he had argued in "Integration," human spatial experience in architecture and landscape are interrelated and continuous; hence it would naturally be better to design house and garden as one. In fact, to do otherwise was just another expression of the institutionalized insanity being inflicted on the environment, as the chapter title "Houses Plus Gardens: The Planned Schizophrenia" in *Creative Gardens* suggests. Objectifying and separating house from garden not only contributed to the disintegration of the physical world; it also made us "insane" by diminishing our perception of our own vital relationship to nature. Fortunately—at least as far as this landscape drama was concerned—on some occasions, such as at his own residence and at the Macht home in Baltimore, Rose had the opportunity to design both house and garden together, and thus to demonstrate the merits of conceiving whole sites in an integrated, spatial way. He called these fusions of house and garden "space-sculptures-with-shelters," suggesting an environmental analogue to the constructivist sculptures whose interlocking spatial qualities had inspired him before the war.[76] In a space-sculpture-with-shelter, a "house" was not an isolated object decorated with landscaping but merely the sheltered part of a larger landscape space, originating from the extant conditions of its site (fig. 17).

Fig. 17. Rose's house and garden, a "space-sculpture-with-shelter," 1954.
Photograph by Lonnie Wasco. Courtesy JRC.

In a patchwork suburban landscape that had been subdivided for the sole purpose of making money—a tactic that Rose described as "dollar planning of the land"—there was almost complete disregard for natural systems and features (even while "nature" was sentimentalized, romanticized, and "preserved" somewhere else) and for the spiritual qualities and practical necessities of life.[77] The destructive result was evident if one merely looked around. "The recipe is simple," Rose sarcastically comments in *Creative Gardens:* "first, spoil the land by slicing it in particles that will bring the most dollars, add any house that has sufficient selling gimmicks to each slice, and garnish with 'landscaping.'"[78]

"Space is the constant in all three-dimensional design," Rose notes in "Plant Forms and Space."[79] In his conception of continuous space integrating shelter, garden, landscape, city, and expanse within nature, Rose saw a cure for the conventional thinking manifested by suburbia. Ever mindful of both the limitations and the possibilities of language, in *Creative Gardens* he observes,

> We do not have an individual word in the American language to describe the fusion of shelter with the landscape, but if the need for it should ever become recognized, we would probably get the word. And who knows? With such a word, we might build a whole community of space-sculpture-with-shelter, instead of houses–plus–gardens. It might even spread to cities, this fusion idea, and then we would have a whole lot of people going from one place to another and carrying on their business and living right in the midst of nature instead of preserving that dream patch of wildflowers somewhere else. It would be like going sane.[80]

Perhaps to preserve his own sanity, Rose escaped suburbia frequently in the 1950s (and thereafter), traveling throughout Europe, northern Africa, and the Middle East, but his invitation to and participation in the World Design Conference in Japan in 1960 enriched his life ever after. Rose became so enamored of Japan that he returned there almost annually—sometimes twice in one year, sometimes for extended periods—until he died in 1991. In Japan's traditional cultural attitude about people and landscape, Rose perceived an antidote to the characteristic American attitude he had come to revile. It is perhaps ironic that the "enemy" island nation at the center of his bitter wartime experience would become a continuous wellspring of consolation and encouragement, providing an exemplar to reinforce his transcendentalist beliefs. However, notwithstanding his admiration for the Japanese expression of the integration of human beings and nature in gardens (and elsewhere), and despite the growing popularity of Japanese gardens in the United States at that time, Rose, who had opposed adapting European precedents in the 1930s, vehemently rejected the idea of trying to re-create Japanese garden forms in 1960s America. As he comments in his second book, *Gardens Make Me Laugh* (1965), "A Japanese garden is a garden made in Japan. . . . There's no such thing as a garden where its people aren't. That's a *translation,* not a garden."[81]

Still, even before he went to Japan, Rose's gardens were often called "Japanese," a fact that roiled him considerably—"the way pimples bother an adolescent," as he put it.[82] Rose's dynamic, obtuse-angled, free-form garden spaces of the 1950s and 1960s did not imitate Japanese garden forms. What they *did* do was provide Rose's clients in America with an opportunity to perceive their integration with nature, such as Japanese designers had succeeded in providing in Japan, though in a necessarily very different way. While Rose certainly respected Japanese gardens, what he understood as their nonspatial character disqualified them, in his opinion, as arbiters of man and nature for contemporary Westerners. In *Gardens Make Me Laugh,* essentially an essay devoted to a comparison of Western and Japanese attitudes about nature (with concise but expressive illustrations by Robert C. Osborn), Rose remarks, "The Japanese garden has modulation and depth, but it is essentially a pictorial experience like a painting—without in-ness, the state of being *in* something. You are 'at' it. And the immediacy of getting 'in' is an additional step of projection which is philosophical or psychological rather than physical." As he describes the Japanese landscape, "It's illusory, not immediate. . . . It's nature painting, not a landscape. It represents something, it's never the thing itself"[83] (fig. 18).

Fig. 18. "Dry stream" as path and storm water management device, Klaiman garden, Saddle River, NJ, c. 1983. Courtesy JRC.

For Rose, as for any modern Westerner, getting "in" a garden philosophically or psychologically could not work on its own; the perception of integration could be achieved only through the immediacy of being physically within the garden space. A keen observer, Rose felt it more instructive to watch the Japanese people themselves; how they moved through the landscape, in particular, helped him understand their gardens. "I don't look at GARDENS," he asserts in *Gardens Make Me Laugh*. "I look at the people, how they walk. You'd be surprised what you can tell about their gardens from the way the people walk—the way they do anything—serve the table, drive a car, greet each other, look at a child."[84]

As his love for Japan grew, Rose became a practitioner of Zen Buddhism, a philosophical point of view compatible with his transcendental roots, his still-evolving spontaneous method of design, and his conception of complex, ever-changing space. In a 1983 interview with Michael Van Valkenburgh, Rose reaffirmed the garden's spiritual purpose in integrating people with nature, as well as the importance of designing space to encourage it:

> Some people think I go to Japan to sneak a peek at the Japanese gardens. I don't. I go to look at the people. They are the garden. My gardens are intended to help my clients with their own self-discovery. A garden is the gateless gate of Zen Buddhism. A garden owner cannot really enter this garden unless he has this understanding. But the way you organize and define space can help people enter the gateless gate.[85]

In his 1960s gardens, as well as in those he made thereafter, Rose became even more focused on his objective of creating the opportunity for an acute perception of nature through designed spatial experiences. Gardens might still provide for the social life of the suburban family, but they *had* to provide for the spiritual reunion of each suburbanite with nature. A typical garden's program might include tennis, swimming, and outdoor dining, but the garden's real purpose was simply to be there when one entered it, so that a fusion of the individual with the infinite might occur. More important for Rose, each garden provided him with the opportunity to ignore or outfox the limitations imposed by authority—to dwell in a creative world where he could engage the physical qualities of a site with minimal interference. Of course, there was always the client. And though Rose recognized clients as important actors in the landscape drama he was directing, he chose not to recognize their proprietary right to decide ultimately what would happen on the land they owned; thus, "moving" the client often became an important part of making the garden. While this approach worked with many people, it sometimes resulted in conflicts and certainly limited Rose's client base (fig. 19).

Rose used his third book, *Modern American Gardens*, to express "How to See a Garden in our changing times." The book begins with a definition of "ecology" and asserts

Fig. 19. "When I say YOU, I mean the sergeant in us all. . . . When *he* struts through the landscape, sparrows fall and raindrops come to attention." Linocut or woodcut print by Rose, c. 1964. From *Modern American Gardens* (1967).

that its readers will discover that "the message of man's relation to his environment is unmistakable. As a result, How to See the landscape at our doorstep becomes at once personal and universal."[86] *Modern American Gardens* includes hundreds of photographs of Rose's 1960s projects but contains neither plans nor drawings, as his gardens were more and more often spontaneously conceived and simultaneously built. That is not to say that there were no plans or models, or any forethought, but an ever-increasing level of direct improvisation was becoming integral to Rose's process. He experienced, designed, and built all at once and in a sequence, proceeding through a site with few preconceptions, much as others would ultimately experience the garden.

In *Modern American Gardens,* Rose uses photographs of his gardens in relation to a sometimes mystical "caption story," written by Rose, to describe how one moves through his designed sequence of landscape spatial experiences, ignoring the "gestalt" that plans would provide. The photographs and caption story are interwoven with what Rose, in the book's introduction, characterizes as Snow's "uncannily perceptive" description of Rose's working methods, as well as Snow's insightful explanation of the modern movement in landscape architecture. Rose's literary and photographic collage describing how to see a garden is itself an experimental form for a book on gardens, not unlike the mosaic that is William Carlos Williams's epic modern American poem *Paterson,* in which one person's fusion with that New Jersey industrial city is communicated through the juxtaposition of narrative, letters, poems, and newspaper clippings.

That "Marc Snow" was brought in as the author of this book is a result of Rose's publisher's dissatisfaction with the incendiary character of his writing in his first book. It is no wonder that Snow could be so "uncannily perceptive" since he was actually the literary persona of Rose. Rose later recounted how he hired a student from Columbia to do research for the book but wrote the text himself; when Rose submitted the manuscript to his publisher, he contrived the name "Marc Snow" as a "snow job."[87] But Rose, for whom it may be said a creative story rooted in facts was truer than just the bare facts, also offered another story to explain his choice of pen name. In his first letter home to his mother after enlisting in the navy, Rose used "snow in April" to describe both his own unusual character and how he planned to passively "just be there" during the war. It appears likely that the simile of "snow in April" stayed in his mind and later inspired the name "March Snow," a character in some of his unpublished short stories. Writing about the name in the afterword to his last book, *The Heavenly Environment—A Landscape Drama in Three Acts with a Backstage Interlude,* Rose describes it as symbolizing "that time of year which can't seem to make up its mind whether to become spring or remain winter. This happens every year in Pennsylvania: just when you believe that spring is here at last, the most enchanting snowfall covers the landscape with a white so pure you don't mind waiting for spring."[88]

When Rose needed an author to cover for *Modern American Gardens,* "March Snow" became "Marc Snow." As Rose tells it in *The Heavenly Environment,* on reading Snow's text, Rose's thoroughly impressed publisher pompously asked Rose why he couldn't write like that, and Rose gave a typically glib response: "'My name isn't Marc Snow,' I said, and looked bewildered as I muttered a silent prayer to Stanislavski."[89]

In 1969 Rose's mother died, shortly after she and Rose had taken out a loan and implemented a major renovation of their home (figs. 20, 21). The changes at Ridgewood

Fig. 20. Rose and carpenter during roof garden construction, 1970. Courtesy JRC.

Fig. 21. Roof garden, looking north, mid-1970s. Photograph by Don Manza. Courtesy JRC.

reflected Rose's now-established interest in practicing Zen Buddhism and the property's new function as a Zen study center in addition to a residence for Rose and his sister Jean. Rose's studio was converted into a separate apartment and rented out sporadically thereafter. Throughout the 1970s and 1980s Rose kept up his pattern of traveling to Japan and throughout Asia; making suburban gardens, mostly in the northeastern United States; continually reinventing his home in Ridgewood; and writing (though his production of magazine articles had declined precipitously by the mid-1960s). His written output during those decades included unpublished plays and short stories and culminated with *The Heavenly Environment*. In it Rose continues to recount his adventures making gardens in suburbia in stories that contain both his philosophy of design and his often humorous (while also quite serious) confrontations with clients, building inspectors, and others in the cast of the suburban landscape farce. Building on his mosaic approach to bookmaking in *Modern American Gardens,* within the acts of *The Heavenly Environment* he intersperses his narrative with old letters, excerpts from magazine articles, photographs of his projects, and a captioned story line, among other items. No plans. Filled with allusions to the theater and references to Zen perspectives, the landscape drama takes shape when clients, sites, and Rose meet onstage in the suburban cultural milieu. As he described it, "In the landscape drama, the designer is the playwright, and in the backstage of his mind he knows full well he cannot invent characters or situations to his liking, but must deal with both—as they are; it is often in that fine line between what is and what it pretends to be that the landscape drama takes its shape."[90]

In the third act of *The Heavenly Environment,* titled "Poor Man's Royalty," Rose tells the story of his Ridgewood home, which had been reincarnated many times since its original construction in 1952–1953. The mosaic of elements in this act includes an opening poem by Rose, "Sunkenberg, Ah Sunkenberg—the autobiography of a place," adjacent to a photograph of the nearby Ho-Ho-Kus Brook. In the poem, Rose recounts the history of industrialization in the region and the suburban development of Ridgewood from the point of view of the innocent, once-peaceful brook; now polluted, and flooding regularly as it runs through town from the Ramapo Hills toward the Great Falls at Paterson (America's first planned industrial city), the brook must suffer the additional indignation of being blamed for its condition by an oblivious and guilty public.[91] Rose makes it clear that "Sunkenberg" is a pseudonym for Ridgewood, site of his home, and that it is also symbolic of anywhere in suburbia in which precious and potentially inspiring resources like water are treated as a problem. What he leaves unsaid is that Sunkenberg was also the name of Ridgewood's building inspector, with whom he had numerous confrontations. As usual with Rose, the creative was both personal and universal.

To further explicate his ideas and work, Rose made a thirty-minute companion video to *The Heavenly Environment*. In the video, which he titled *The Heavenly Environment and Other Crimes,* Rose emphasizes the culpability of regulations, as well as of irrational social mores, in destroying the possibility for people to experience a "heavenly" natural world and to perceive their part in creation. He rails against the impact of zoning laws and building codes, which he says are "designing the landscape . . . and made by people who are incompetent as designers," and clarifies his defiant, alternative approach to landscape design as "conforming to nature rather than conforming to the absurdities of some zoning law." In an obvious reference to Thoreau, Rose explains his own higher calling by proclaiming, "When confronted by an absurd law, that's the time to resort to civil disobedience."[92]

Rose completed at least eighty-six projects in his last two decades, and he includes a guided tour of several in *The Heavenly Environment and Other Crimes.*[93] More than just built critiques of mindless regulations and conventional behaviors, many offered practical and inspiring solutions to environmental problems that designers today are seeking to address. These are achieved by Rose's skillful manipulation of space, along with a venerable regard for our vital relationship with nature that is made abundantly clear by Rose's concluding the video with an excerpt from Thoreau's poem "Inspiration," as the last of his garden images dissolves onscreen before our eyes:

Always the general show of things
Floats in review before my mind,
And such true love and reverence brings,
That sometimes I forget that I am blind.

The little-known gardens that Rose produced in the
1970s and 1980s for the most part represented an evolution
from his earliest perspectives and remained characteristically
creative, modern, and American, even if an overzealous,
Buddhist-like detail could occasionally be found. In their
celebration of natural resources and their concern with spirituality, the gardens were, like their author, mavericks in
suburbia. Most were built without plans near Rose's home
by contractors he trained, enabling him to have almost continuous and complete control.

On more than thirty of his 1970s and 1980s projects,
Rose collaborated with the architect Eleanore Pettersen.
Pettersen had first heard of James Rose when, as a student at
Cooper Union (1937–1941), she read his *Pencil Points* articles
(fig. 22). As she remembered, "Everyone was reading Jim's
articles then and everyone was very excited by them."[94] She
went on to apprentice for Frank Lloyd Wright at Taliesen
from 1941 to 1943. After the war she worked for the Tennessee Valley Authority and then for the architect Arthur
Rigolo in Clifton, New Jersey, before establishing her own
architectural practice in the early 1950s, becoming the first
woman in New Jersey to do so.

Aside from her willingness to put up with Rose's
prickly personality and unorthodox methods, what probably made Pettersen such a good collaborator during these
years was her respect for the existing conditions of sites
(possibly inspired by her apprenticeship with Wright); her
modern, open spatial sensibility, including an appreciation

Fig. 22. Eleanore Pettersen, 1950s. Photograph by George Peirce. © georgepeirce.com.

for fluency between indoors and out (possibly inspired by Rose's articles); and her "hands-on" approach to architecture. Having brought Rose into projects, she often found herself defending him when clients or officials became frustrated or alienated by his antics. One might think she would have tired of it, yet she persisted, often reminding her clients, "It will be worth it."[95]

During this period Rose typically began each day meditating in the zendo he had constructed on his roof. Here he freed his mind from preconceptions before he went to work directly on the sites. For the most part, he designed spontaneously, using an approach that was flexible enough to respond to whatever conditions and situations he might encounter. Throughout his career Rose recoiled from designing according to preconceived principles, yet as his garden making evolved, certain general themes became manifest and were expressed with increasing authority.

Owing to Rose's method of spontaneous improvisation with and in the landscape, his gardens exhibit a vitality uncommon in most modern professional landscape design; one can almost feel the creative act occurring as one moves sequentially through the spaces (fig. 23). In some cases, gardens ended only when Rose ran out of money or geography (though sometimes even the property line did not stop him), or when his clients ran out of patience. Rose facilitated this

Fig. 23. Maloney garden, Saddle River, NJ, 1993. Photograph by author. Courtesy JRC.

method, one that was unconventional in the modern West, by practicing a unique form of design-build as his work evolved, forging close and sometimes exclusive relationships with carefully cultivated contractors. Rose spent most of his days at his projects, directing the action and making on-the-spot design decisions, which he personally communicated to his foremen. To Rui Barardo and Jose Ferreira, his primary foremen in the 1970s and 1980s, Rose would explain, "I am the eyes, you are the hands."[96]

Rose always made a major effort to minimize disturbance at his sites, a trait evident even in his earliest projects. His urge to conserve site features and systems intensified over time and, together with the techniques he developed, enabled him to intervene in a manner that was both expressive and nondestructive. "People are continually asking me how I design a garden," he commented, "as if I had some kind of formula, and I don't. I do not do anything to prevent them from being alive. They're already alive. It's not something I do. It's already there. I just don't destroy it. It's as simple as that, you see, and people look at it in a different way. They think it's something I do. It's something I don't do. And it's something I prevent them from doing. And then what's there is wonderful."[97]

The same keen eye and creative imagination that helped Rose scavenge materials and reuse them in his Okinawa models and his gardens would inspire him to remove from his sites only those things that were interfering with people's perceptions of their relationship to the land, and to reuse them in less disruptive ways. As his friend George Skrubb insightfully observed after visiting several of Rose's postwar gardens, "I discovered he was searching for what is already there, but hidden by obstacles left by man and nature."[98]

Beyond preserving natural features and systems, Rose

sought to understand the essential quality of each site so that his intervention could more clearly reveal that quality to others. In *The Heavenly Environment* he notes that "there is a quality that is different in every site, a quality that is of the place, not one manufactured or brought in. To find that quality is to allow the place to speak for itself."[99] One excellent example of Rose's highlighting a site's essential quality is the Anisfield garden, which he designed and built in Saddle River, New Jersey, in 1982–1983. Here Rose reused the rocks from an ancient glacial riverbed he found on-site to help him transform a mildly sloping topography into subtle terraces that expressed the site's geologic history and did not disturb the roots of the trees. Plantings of native rhododendron helped to guide the experience through the dappled shade of the mature woodland that had long been established there (fig. 24). Another example is the 1986 Werlin residence in Englewood, New Jersey, where a swampy bottomland was transmuted into a playful water garden using the site's existing impervious soils to redefine a series of pools interlaced with shallow angular terraces that guided movement beneath and around established trees.

At each site Rose incorporated existing features into his palette of materials to define space within which he could inspire others' perceptions of the place. He had revealed his interest in doing so as early as 1941 in his work on the Dickinson residence in Pasadena, California, but saving and engaging existing trees, outcroppings, and other site features became a dominant characteristic of his gardens and was a major determinant of their forms throughout his career. When the grade of a site permitted it, Rose often constructed shallow terraces and steps, angled around the trunks of trees, which created a strong sense of three-dimensional "bas-relief" and interlocking space-form as they guided

Fig. 24. Path and drainage channel, Anisfield garden, Saddle River, NJ, 1991. Photograph by author. Courtesy JRC.

people through the woods without disturbing tree roots. Even on steeper sites, such as the 1956 Macht residence in Baltimore, terraces were established at the grade of existing trees, allowing the trees to be participants in determining the garden space-form.

In addition to incorporating site features where he found them, Rose would often redeploy rocks and plants he discovered on-site to define space with materials expressive of the site's native character. Rose described an example of this at the 1974 Paley garden in Saddle River, New Jersey: "Without bringing in a lot of new material or new stuff, as the construction work went on a lot of things that were already there revealed themselves, as, for instance, the enormous rocks you have seen. None of these were brought in to have rocks as a possession. They were simply there, and rather than digging a hole to bury them so you can have a nice lawn or something like that, we used them. We rearranged them, put them where they would create space and make what people are now calling a garden."[100]

The dominant characteristic of Rose's planting design was his decision to work with the vegetation already present, carefully weaving space through and around trees or rearranging plants to make each site's character more accessible (fig. 25). His urge to preserve existing trees was so powerful that he even maintained those that were unhealthy or ugly by conventional standards, especially when they served a spatial purpose. One such case was an old decaying willow in the Tremaine garden in Paramus, New Jersey, created by Rose in 1984. To most people the tree was an eyesore, but it helped to provide privacy, an essential component of all gardens. Nonetheless, everyone wanted it removed. An arborist assessed the tree as dying, and as dangerous to boot, and insisted that it should be taken out, to which Rose snapped

Fig. 25. Passage from parking area through woods to house, Germano garden, Saddle River, NJ, 1993.
Photograph by Karen Krolewski. Courtesy JRC.

back, "Would you take the lion out of the circus?"[101] The willow stayed, and privacy was maintained.

As his work evolved, when Rose did need to import plants to contribute to the creation of his design, he brought in cheap, readily available ones, usually native species. He used very few species of new plants in his space-sculptures. Almost never was there any lawn. Ever frugal, he would sometimes dig mountain laurel from his Pennsylvania property or recycle overgrown plants from one job to reuse on another. Rose's understanding and appreciation of plants as distinctive living materials that make space in unique, sculptural ways was evident as early as 1939, when he wrote:

> Plants . . . require deeper knowledge and experience in their use than any other material. For example, to use plants intelligently, a landscaper must first

know his territory: soil, climate, and indigenous growth. Then he must understand plant forms: not as he would like to have them (or as he might draw them) but as they grow, and to what extent they can be found in variations from the type, or altered and directed by constructive pruning. He must understand the potentialities of each plant: rate of growth, maximum height and breadth, and characteristic effect at maturity. He must know them not as separate forms alone, but also the immaterial form which will result in combination with other living and architectural materials. . . . He must visualize the constant change due to growth and season, and arrange for combinations which, as they change, will create an evolving space effect analogous to recent experiments in sculpture which preserve plastic and interspatial effects while in motion.[102]

Likewise, when Rose brought in new building materials he used only a few. The gridded, exposed aggregate concrete and permeable blacktop used for paving in his earlier built work, such as the Macht residence in Baltimore and the 1959 Averett residence in Columbus, Georgia, gave way to mosaics of broken Pennsylvania bluestone, cobbles, pebbles, and rocks found on-site in later projects such as the Anisfield residence in Saddle River and the 1987 Glickman residence in Allendale, New Jersey. In many later projects, including the 1982 Van Ness residence in Saddle River, Rose—perhaps inspired by the pagoda-shaped lanterns he saw in Japan—assembled leftover pieces of Pennsylvania bluestone into layered stone lanterns. Found boulders were sometimes used in his "rock ikebana" accents, as at the Paley residence and on many other sites. Railroad ties or (late in his career, when ties became less readily available) landscape timbers were used for steps and walls as well as for benches and other garden structures. Rose often used leftover copper roof flashing or other scrap sheet metal for lanterns and fountains, beginning with his 1960 G-V Controls courtyard in Livingston, New Jersey. Such scrap metal sculpture can be seen today at the James Rose Center.

Form in these gardens was created by the natural conditions of the sites and by Rose's own refined spatial sensibility. Rarely was there any evidence of his clients' formal or material preferences. The always different obtuse-angled segments, often resulting from Rose's materials, replaced the grid entirely in his later gardens and gave him the flexibility to engage his sites sequentially. They allowed for changes in direction, focus, and intensification and for attenuation in guiding the spatial experience. Specific space-form could result spontaneously in response to the particulars of the site, as Rose sought an equilibrium between the character and natural features of the land and his own spatial interventions, thus making spaces within which he and his clients could become more aware of nature.

While patterns and textures were always part of the spatial experience, color had no place in Rose's space-sculptures. There is evidence that Rose may have had some difficulty seeing color when he was young, but it is unlikely that this played much of a role in his obsession with space and light.[103] In any case, Rose had no reservations about resisting any attempt to introduce color into his masterpieces. When he noticed during a visit to the Van Ness garden that someone had had the effrontery to plant pink and purple impatiens at the base of some trees, he remarked in disgust, "It's like painting a mustache on the Mona Lisa!"[104]

Last, and perhaps most significant, Rose's gardens were

designed with a mature and profound awareness of change. His gardens changed as one moved through them. They changed daily, seasonally, and over longer periods, and they changed with the changes that happen within everyone as they live and grow. This recognition of the essential nature of change was profound in Rose and his gardens. "Change is the essence," he writes in *The Heavenly Environment*. "To reveal what is always there is the trick. The metamorphosis is seen minute by minute, season by season, year by year. Through this looking glass, 'finish' is another word for death" (fig. 26).[105]

In his postwar career Rose produced books and gardens that were the antithesis of the environmental degradation and spiritual vacuum he perceived in suburbia. His work provided him with a personal refuge and the opportunity to share a transcendent experience with others. For Rose, the transformation of suburbia would begin not with the

Fig. 26. Pool at Ridgewood, 1999. Courtesy JRC.

corrupt institutions that created it but within individuals. In his gardens, his frugal practicality and creative spirit translated into an evolving modern design aesthetic that incorporated both conservation and spiritual values. In his books, he strove to find a way to elevate words—which so often obscure the essential nonverbal message of landscape—to art, and he often succeeded. Rose continued working on his gardens and books almost until the day he died, leaving behind a half-finished project in Short Hills and an idea for a fifth book that he imagined as nothing but captions placed perfectly on the white space of its pages.

Epilogue

James Rose died from liver cancer on September 16, 1991. During his lifetime his home in Ridgewood had become the physical manifestation of the "little island in the mind" he had discovered during the war: a real place of equilibrium that he could perpetually reinvent as things inevitably changed around and within him. By the end of his life, however, his home, conceived of and built to accommodate rapid change, had fallen into disrepair. Neglect, vandalism, and "temporary" construction techniques, as well as fire and water damage, had all taken their toll. Roofs and pools were leaking, two-by-fours propped up ceiling joists, windows were broken or missing, mechanical systems no longer functioned, siding was rotting, once-delicate woven fences had collapsed, inventive furnishings had rusted, plants were taking over. Raccoons had begun sleeping in the zendo, and teenagers from the high school came to smoke behind the bushes, unconsciously drawn to Rose's outlaw lair.

All of his books were out of print; most of his early gardens, as well as some of the more recent ones, were gone, with not much to remember them by. Suburbia had continued to swallow up and lay waste to the remaining land around him, all but eradicating the sense of place Rose had sought to preserve and help others perceive in creative, modern, heavenly gardens of space and light. Somewhere, Sunkenberg was laughing.

In the years immediately before his death, Rose and a few friends established a nonprofit foundation to assist with contemporary issues in landscape architecture education and practice.[106] To the foundation (and the raccoons) Rose left his home and legacy. The James Rose Center for Landscape Architectural Research and Design has since maintained this unique home as its headquarters, continuously striving to rehabilitate it while opening it to the public seasonally and for special events (fig. 27). The Center has documented many of Rose's works that survived into the 1990s, recording them in drawings and black-and-white photographs of which Rose would probably not approve. In addition, the Center engages contemporary suburban environmental design issues and problems through research, outreach, and service programs grounded in Rose's insights about space, spirit, and ecology.

Rooted in the soil along the Delaware River, inspired by modern art and culture, disillusioned by the war, and determined to live creatively and in harmony with the earth, throughout the arc of his life and work Rose was always disrespectful of authority and of the mindless conformity it seemed to demand. It is little surprise that his legacy has been almost invisible. Onstage in modern America, his acutely critical, brash, and often confrontational persona disguised and protected a vulnerable and sentient

Fig. 27. James Rose Center, looking west from eastern property line, 1996.
Photograph by Frederick Charles. © fcharles.com.

soul capable of exquisite gardens and eloquent passages that were the antithesis of the times in which he lived, even as they were shaped by them.

Perhaps through the efforts of the James Rose Center, maverick Rose's legacy is beginning to be felt. But if noth-

Fig. 28. Rose, early 1980s. Courtesy JRC.

ing else, his rebellious life and work hopefully will inspire those who can see Rose between the cracks of history: a portrait of the creative spirit in a life lived defiantly against the tide of modern American conformity, providing a tracery of that modern world, too, through the "transparent but impenetrable screen" of time and change.

View from living area to terrace, Dickinson garden and house, 1946. Photograph by Julius Shulman. © J. Paul Getty Trust. Getty Research Institute, Los Angeles.

DICKINSON GARDEN
AND HOUSE

PASADENA, CALIFORNIA

(1941)

In 1940–1941 James Rose spent much of his brief stay in California writing articles and giving lectures, continuing the theoretical exploration of modern landscape design in which he had been engaged on the East Coast. The nature of fluid modern landscape space and its fusion with open architectural space remained central to his thought, as expressed in his 1940 *California Arts and Architecture* article "Gardens":

> We no longer set up special compartments in our houses—the parlor (with shades drawn to save the mohair upholstery), the drawing room, the dining room. We are already accustomed to a freer type of space organization—living-dining rooms with groups arranged for conversation, study, and play. This has the obvious advantage of less bulk to take care of, but it is only the beginning. We have yet to develop the house and landscape unit on the same

basis rather than just the house with the garden attached.[1]

Paid design commissions were harder to find, but in the residence of Mrs. Thompson Dickinson, Rose, perhaps for the first time, had the opportunity to express, in a built work, modern design themes he had been devising and champi-

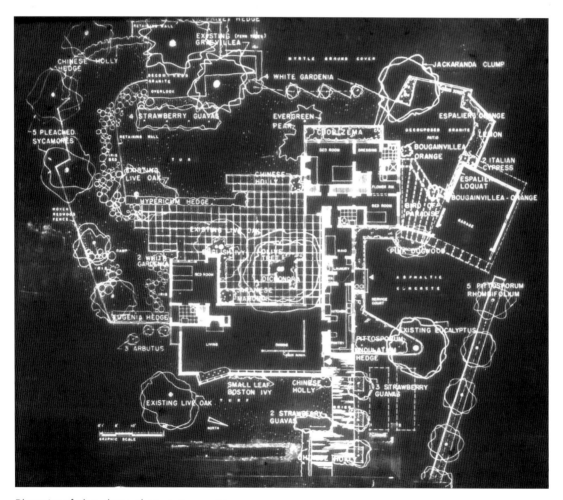

Blueprint of plan, date unknown. Courtesy JRC.

oning with words and in models. Here Rose created a fluid landscape space, challenging the separation of suburban house from garden as he worked side by side with the architect Lawrence Test and designer Woodbridge Dickinson Jr., who was the client's son.[2] Rose's use of flexible, inexpensive modular paving at the Dickinson residence foreshadows his fuller examination of modular landscape design that would come right after the war, as well as his general interest in engaging the grid as a tactic for interlocking inside and out, a device he would continue to employ in future commissions.[3] Rose also began to experiment with an asymmetrical, non-orthogonal geometry that could respond to existing site conditions in an original way, a geometry that would grow into his trademark obtuse-angled "space-form" as his work evolved.

In his book *Creative Gardens* (1958), Rose notes that the Dickinson site "was in an already well-developed section. The plot, a truncated wedge, sloped gently and evenly from the curving street to an abrupt drop into an arroyo in the rear. At the edge of this precipice were two magnificent fern trees (Grevillea): beyond, a distant backdrop of snow-capped peaks."[4] The house was designed in a partial U-shape, thereby beginning to contain the garden space within its wings while providing privacy from passersby and neighbors. Additional privacy and spatial definition for the garden were achieved by planting a row of pleached sycamores and constructing a fence along the eastern property line, helping to orient the unified space over the arroyo and toward the mountain views. From the street, the integrated "house and landscape unit" was designed to look "severe, but friendly," as Rose put it. On entering the property, one was offered a sense of what he called the "interspatial feeling of the gardens beyond," supported in part by a space-dividing row of strawberry guavas that was repeated in the terraces at the rear of the house.[5]

Front of residence, 1946. Photograph by Julius Shulman. © J. Paul Getty Trust. Getty Research Institute, Los Angeles.

The main living space inside the house was separated from the rear terraces only by a series of continuous sliding glass doors, thus enabling a feeling of flexible and integrated indoor–outdoor space. This was reinforced by a grid of modular, acid-etched, exposed aggregate concrete terrace pavers running beneath the glass doors and into the house along the hall on its northwestern side. The continuous space of house-and-garden, circumscribed on three sides, was interrupted by plantings (including the guavas and a transplanted specimen olive tree) or by furniture (such as the piano), as boulders might interrupt the flow of water in a stream. As Rose would later explain, "The design of both the house and the landscape were approached under ideal conditions of collaboration between the architect and landscape architect.

A modular concrete grid joins outdoors and indoors. Photograph by Julius Shulman, 1946. © J. Paul Getty Trust. Getty Research Institute, Los Angeles.

The heart of the scheme lies in the complete spatial integration of the exterior and interior. The series of terraces across the entire southwest face of the house, which traditionally would have been segregated and distributed over vast areas, were fused into a single interspatial unit having total immediacy with the house."[6]

This series of three shallow terraces possessed "total immediacy with the house" and, at least visually, with the distant landscape as well, culminating in what *Architectural*

Rear of residence, 1946. Photograph by Julius Shulman. © J. Paul Getty Trust. Getty Research Institute, Los Angeles.

Forum described as "the scheme's *chef d'oeuvre*—the 'over-look' beneath the fern trees."[7] Rose's integration of existing site features and conditions, such as the fern trees and the views, was certainly not unprecedented in landscape design, but it is noteworthy nonetheless, as the specific conditions of his sites would increasingly come to play a dominant role in determining the character and form of his interventions.

An asymmetrical, obtuse-angled gravel patio, designed to support the gardening activities of Mrs. Dickinson,

View across terraces toward overlook, 1946. Photograph by Julius Shulman. © J. Paul Getty Trust. Getty Research Institute, Los Angeles.

Gardening patio. Photograph by Julius Shulman, 1946. © J. Paul Getty Trust. Getty Research Institute, Los Angeles.

extended from a small wedge of space between the master bedroom suite and the garage. Linked to a zigzag path near the edge of the arroyo, the patio was partly defined by two interlocking screens, one opaque and one glazed with clear glass to frame those mountain views southwest of the garden while protecting the patio from the winds rising from the arroyo. In Rose's use of these screens one is reminded of Christopher Tunnard and Serge Chermayeff's use of a partially glazed screen to frame views at Bentley Wood in East

Glazed screen between gardening patio and arroyo. Photograph by Julius Shulman, 1946. © J. Paul Getty Trust. Getty Research Institute, Los Angeles.

Sussex, England, several years earlier, a project with which Rose was undoubtedly familiar.[8] However, at the Dickinson site, taking an approach that was very different from the orthogonal view-framing screens at Bentley Wood, Rose experimented with the "freer" possibilities of an asymmetrical, non-orthogonal geometry to make flexible modern landscape space responsive to site features and materials. This obtuse-angled spatial geometry would perhaps more than anything else come to characterize Rose's work, providing him almost unlimited opportunity to preserve and engage extant site conditions, whatever they might be.

The Dickinson residence was first published in *Architectural Forum* in November 1946, with beautiful black-and-white photographs by Julius Shulman. As if to emphasize that modern landscape design was not about plants as much as it was about space, Rose, at the magazine's request, suggested substitute plantings appropriate for the northeastern United States which would maintain the spatial character of the design in that climate. Rose himself published this project under the title "Pasadena" in *Creative Gardens,* where he supplements Shulman's images with an axonometric plan drawn by Charles Rieger as well as with his own sketches and written description.

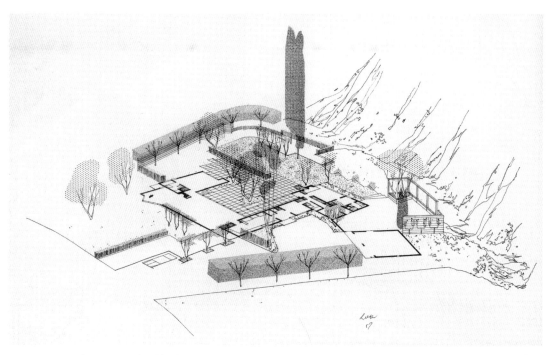

Axonometric plan. Drawn by Charles Rieger. From *Creative Gardens* (1958).

Today little is left of the "severe, but friendly" view in the front of the property. No hint of the "interspatial feeling of the gardens beyond" remains, as Rose's simple, well-scaled planting scheme has been replaced by decorative foundation plantings and small boulders. In the rear, his irregular patio and screens, the adjacent zigzag path, and the extant fern trees are also gone. Indeed, almost none of the original space-dividing and space-defining plantings survive, and the terraces have been modified. However, within the house and above the arroyo, although it is muddled some by boulders and small "gardens," the singular, interspatial "house and landscape unit" with its integrating grid of flexible modular paving, interrupted by the original transplanted olive tree, can still be experienced—a memorial to Rose, Test, and Dickinson's collaborative concern to create almost seamless modern indoor–outdoor space.

In its expression of Rose's early design thinking, including the fluid and continuous spatial relationship between inside and out, the Dickinson residence initiated an iterative process between theory and practice that would characterize Rose's almost fifty-year career of writing about and making landscapes. Moreover, it served as precedent, giving early form to Rose's fundamental design concerns in ways that would reappear—even as they were edited, refined, and adjusted—in hundreds of subsequent commissions. Perhaps this was nowhere more evident than in Rose's gridded site design for his own family home, a project over which he had virtually complete control of both architecture and landscape (not to mention client). The residence of Jean Gillmor and James and Minnie Rose in New Jersey was conceived of shortly after the California Dickinson residence was built, but under quite different circumstances, thousands of miles away on a Pacific island.

Rose at work in western courtyard at Ridgewood, 1953. Courtesy JRC.

ROSE GARDEN AND HOUSE

RIDGEWOOD, NEW JERSEY

(PART 1: 1944–1968)

Passing time between military tasks on Okinawa in the waning months of 1944, James Rose imagined a modern landscape—complete with house—for himself, his mother, Minnie Rose, and his sister, Jean Gillmor, making a model of it out of scraps he scavenged from construction battalion headquarters. To the dismay of local planning authorities and building inspectors, his dream home was eventually built in 1952–1953 on a leftover parcel of land at an old trolley stop along the Ho-Ho-Kus Brook in the New York City suburb of Ridgewood, New Jersey.[1] As Rose, using the third person, describes his objectives in a brochure he created for an open house in 1953, "Mr. Rose designed the original model while on Okinawa during World War II. He has attempted to group three separate and complete units, supplying a maximum of privacy and space with a minimum of housekeeping."[2]

Foreshadowed in his *Pencil Points* and *California Arts*

and Architecture articles, constructed in a postwar suburbia he reviled, and continuously reinvented over almost four decades, Rose's magnum opus provides us with an unusually comprehensive record of the mind of one of landscape architecture's most visionary modern thinkers and designers, as well as an alternative image of what America's suburbs could have been, and perhaps still can be. In its rich expression of a small house and landscape as a single modern spatial unit, its integration with a mundane suburban site, and especially its premeditated embrace of change, Rose's Ridgewood home was both a personal dream come true and a built critique of the American Dream.

In an article he wrote for the October 1946 issue of *American Home* magazine, Rose reflects on his state of mind while building the model: "It was the kind of dream the prisoners dreamed when, eating roots, they devised elaborate menus with hollandaise sauce and other fancy trimmings. . . . I didn't have a site, or materials. I didn't know that I would ever build. But twelve thousand miles from home those things are not important. It's the idea that counts."[3] After citing his unsettling wartime experiences in confirming the importance of efficiently organized space and the necessity for privacy, he resolves "to plan the house and garden as an integrated whole," determining that both architectural and landscape elements should be conceived together "in a structure based upon a dimensional unit directly related to living needs." In Rose's imagined minimalist house-and-garden structure, any waste or material luxury would be eschewed in favor of what he understood as true luxury, achieved by "arriving at a minimum that will house the activity and leave a maximum feeling of free space . . . and the simplest way of doing this is by making the landscape part of the house."[4]

As if his hope to achieve all this was not ambitious

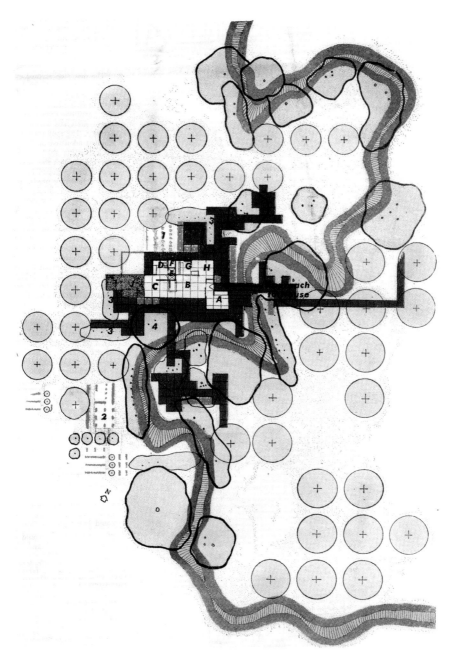

Connecticut site plan of Rose house and garden (unbuilt). From *American Home* (October 1946).

enough, Rose describes a flexible design so married with the natural features of its site that the resulting fusion will create a new, living thing, one that will grow and change over time. He explains his structural vision phenomenally as an analogue to modern sculpture that is grounded in the dynamics of its site:

> I wanted a structural pattern as plastic as good sculpture—large and open enough to wander through. I wanted to be able to wonder whether I was indoors or out on fine, cool days, and yet be snugly insulated from the heat and cold. I wanted the sensations one feels when passing from concrete paving to pine needles and earth. . . . I wanted the spaces flowing easily from one to another, divided for privacy and for convenience. I wanted the arrangement flexible and varied. Most of all, I wanted all this integrated with

Sketch illustrating continuity between indoors and outdoors. From *American Home* (October 1946).

the site in a design that seemed to grow, to mature, to renew itself as all living things do.[5]

Rose goes on to explain that "the design never came to life until I found a site along a meandering stream in Connecticut," prompting him to transform his preliminary vision. He concludes the *American Home* article with a description of the transformed design's characteristics, providing a schematic site plan and perspective sketches to illustrate how this integrated vision of gridded interior and exterior space would fuse with the features of this particular site, especially its meandering stream. But Rose's anticipated purchase of the Connecticut land fell through, and his vision would not truly "come to life" until a short time later, when his family came into possession of an unwanted, awkwardly proportioned 10,000-square-foot "scrap" of land in Ridgewood, New Jersey (near where his mother and sister had been renting). Perhaps ironically, such a tiny, overlooked parcel in a well-established, traditional American suburb would prove to be a fertile, if at times inhospitable, location for his dream home.

In *Creative Gardens* Rose describes his approach to building at the site: "I decided to go at the construction as you might a painting or a piece of sculpture. I set up the basic armature of walls, and roofs, and open spaces to establish their relationships, but left it free in detail to allow for improvisation. In that way it would never be 'finished,' but constantly evolving from one stage to the next—a metamorphosis such as we find, commonly, in nature."[6] Armed with the conviction that "space is the constant in all three-dimensional design," at his own home Rose erased the lines that traditionally separated architect, landscape architect, sculptor, interior designer, and furniture maker, along with those lines separating inside from out. Here he designed and organized everything, since every "thing" contributed to the forming of a unified but flexible space through which he and his family would "circulate and carry on the functions of modern living."[7]

Soon after it was built, Rose's home appeared in an article published in *Progressive Architecture* in December 1954, where it was juxtaposed with a traditional Japanese house and garden constructed in the courtyard of New York's Museum of Modern Art.[8] The Japanese house was modeled after sixteenth- and seventeenth-century prototypes and designed by the architect Junzo Yoshimura, who, like Rose, had worked for Antonin Raymond in Pennsylvania before the war. It was first built in Nagoya, Japan, and then reassembled in the courtyard of MoMA. The garden, designed by Yoshimura and Tansai Sano with the help of a consultant, Ethelbert Furlong, represents a Buddhist image of paradise, with heaven symbolized by a mountain in water. *Progressive Architecture* titled Yoshimura's design "A Traditional Japanese House: The Esthetic Discipline" and the Rose home "A Contemporary American House: The Spatial Discipline." In comparing the two projects, the article points out how modern Western architectural ideas—such as appreciation for the aesthetic quality of the structural system, house plan flexibility, and a close indoor–outdoor relationship—were anticipated in the traditional Japanese design.[9] The Rose home, an efficiently and intricately woven environment for three related adults, is lauded for fusing landscape and architectural spaces while providing complete independence and privacy for its residents. Significantly, unlike the Japanese garden in the museum courtyard, which was meant to be viewed from the house, the outdoor spaces of Rose's spatially integrated home, like the indoor ones with which they were fused, were meant to be physically inhabited.

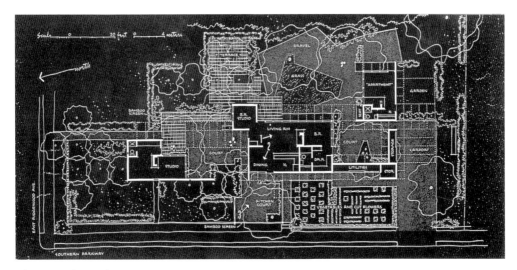

Blueprint of site plan. From *Progressive Architecture* (December 1954).

View north showing integrated structural pattern, 1954. Courtesy JRC.

Japanese garden at the Museum of Modern Art, New York, 1954. Photograph by Ezra Stoller. © Ezra Stoller/Esto.

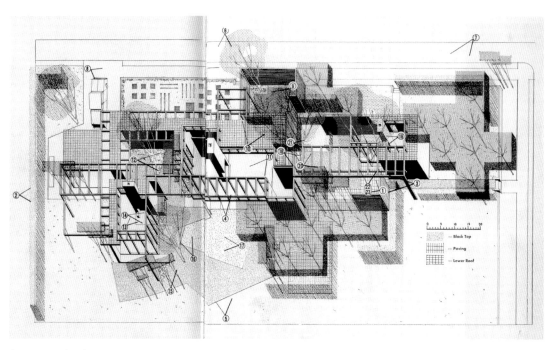

Axonometric plan. Drawn by Charles Rieger. From *Creative Gardens*.

The *Progressive Architecture* article outlines important aspects of Rose's dream home, but its description of the outdoor spaces as "extensions" of the indoor ones is misleading, suggesting that Rose began with an architectural spatial conception and then extended it outdoors to the landscape. As Rose had promised in his journal and magazine articles, his spatial parti for "house" and "garden" at Ridgewood was one unit—a single, three-dimensional, gridded design concept for an entire site, within which the "house" was merely the sheltered part. The article in *Progressive Architecture* also fails to point out the importance to Rose of fusing his gridded spatial concept with his tiny site's significant if humble features, including two American lindens, two ailanthus, and two cherries.

At Ridgewood, Rose's three-dimensional grid, constructed of simple materials, was juxtaposed with the spatial patterns of existing trees, which were sometimes highlighted by obtuse-angled paving forms—not merely to preserve them but also to create a fully integrated spatial experience that was grounded in its site conditions here, as it would have been in Connecticut. Rose's unifying grid and tree concept for his family's home enabled conventional ideas about "house" and "garden" to fuse into something new, and the distinction between "indoors" and "outdoors" to dissolve in a continuous dynamic space. As he would later pronounce, it was "neither landscape nor architecture but both; neither indoors nor outdoors, but both; . . . that may be the message held in the emptiness between the lines drawn by materials."[10]

Rose goes to great lengths in *Creative Gardens* to describe his vision as it was first realized on his tiny Ridgewood site, using twenty-three mostly large-format black-and-white photographs by Lionel Freedman and Lonnie Wasco that are carefully keyed to a stylized, axonometric plan drawn

Concrete block edges the northern shelter and landscape and is used in paving, table tops, and walls.
Photograph by Lonnie Wasco. From *Progressive Architecture* (1954).

by Charles Rieger. The text, however, is pure Rose, as he describes, with characteristic irony and wit, the act of trying to build such an unconventional home in "patchwork" American suburbia; in so doing, he exposes his literary and dramatic proclivities, comparing people experiencing the spaces within his home to characters in a Chekhov play for whom "artificial poses were impossible."[11] The result is Rose-theater—modern environmental satire—with Rose in the roles of both playwright and protagonist taking obvious pleasure in confronting and outfoxing suburban authority and conventional thinking.

In *Creative Gardens* Rose describes his home as a "tiny village," pointing out that the entire building area of his site (after taking setbacks into consideration) was only slightly larger than half a tennis court. Here he occupied a private studio on the north of the property, while his mother lived in the central part of the dwelling, and his sister resided in the

View from northern shelter to landscape. Photograph by Lonnie Wasco. From *Progressive Architecture* (1954).

apartment on the south. Each sheltered volume was designed to provide everything needed for private living, sleeping, and bathing, including a space-dividing fireplace, but only Minnie's shelter contained space for cooking and communal gatherings. Besides the private shelters, the design included terraces, courtyards, and a vegetable and cutting garden, as well as a carport, a driveway, and walkways.

The shelters were fused with the courtyards and gardens throughout the site and up to the property lines. Rose achieved this fusion in part by deconstructing the idea of the single-family house as a solitary object, almost literally pulling it apart to form both the three private shel-

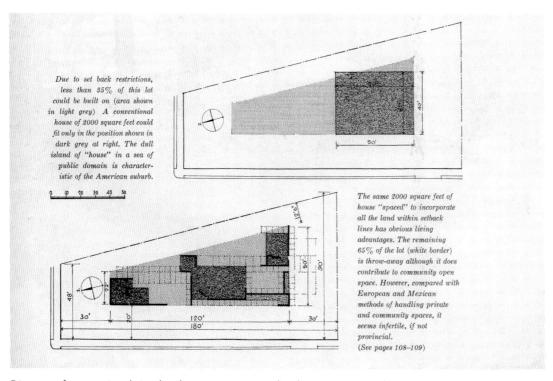

Due to set back restrictions, less than 35% of this lot could be built on (area shown in light grey) A conventional house of 2000 square feet could fit only in the position shown in dark grey at right. The dull island of "house" in a sea of public domain is characteristic of the American suburb.

The same 2000 square feet of house "spaced" to incorporate all the land within setback lines has obvious living advantages. The remaining 65% of the lot (white border) is throw-away although it does contribute to community open space. However, compared with European and Mexican methods of handling private and community spaces, it seems infertile, if not provincial.
(See pages 108–109)

Diagram of conventional site development juxtaposed with Rose's approach. From *Creative Gardens* (1958).

View from central shelter to eastern courtyard. From *Progressive Architecture* (1954).

ters and a series of three interstitial courtyards that both
united and separated them. Sheltered spaces and integral
landscape courtyards were united by floor-to-ceiling glass
walls (making the small shelters feel larger and part of the
landscape), while concrete block walls, often with cleresto-
ries, provided the three occupants with privacy from each
other as well as from the surrounding streets and neighbors. Additional privacy and spatial definition was created
by bamboo screens, white pine hedges, and other plant-

ings on the grid, including numerous white birches. The framework of the buildings' roofs extended, weblike, over portions of the tree-perforated courtyards, further stitching together inside and out. These trellis-like structures provided Rose a kind of overhead stage from which he would soon experiment with hanging ephemeral spatial improvisations.[12] In Rose's flexible space-sculpture-with-shelter, treating the architecture as an integral part of the site grid enabled him to use the existing trees (as well as newly planted ones) to further define the space, modulate the climate, and mediate the incoming light.

In Miesian fashion, Rose extended the concrete block walls defining the sheltered spaces beyond the planes of intersecting glass to begin to define the courtyards as well.[13] As he explains in *Creative Gardens,* "I think the experiment illustrates both the spatial and esthetic increment of the fusion [of architecture and landscape]. The walls become garden walls instead of barriers. The landscape is of the house instead of attached to it, and the space is one."[14]

In places, Rose also extended the interior fir ceilings through the glass walls, and everywhere he adjusted the ground plane so that the many thresholds between inside and out were flush, despite the challenges that the New Jersey climate posed to such an approach. Within the shelters the floor was a heated concrete slab. Outside ground surfaces included asphalt, a well-defined irregular lawn, crushed brick, and concrete block pavers that in their composition, patterning, and surface dimension mimicked the adjacent interpenetrating concrete block walls of house-and-garden. Rose even designed metal-framed tables using these same block pavers and he placed them in the courtyards. He also employed seating that could be used in both the courtyards and the shelters. Rose had designed the woven plastic cord

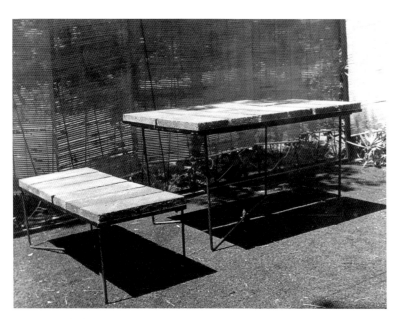

Concrete block and steel tables, 1954. Courtesy JRC.

chairs and benches for other landscape projects in the late 1940s, likely inspired by the weaving activities of his mother and sister (whose loom was also visible in the integrated space). The use of these chairs and benches on both sides of the transparent glass walls conjoining shelter and courtyard here helped reinforce the oneness of the space.[15]

Soon after moving in, Rose began the improvisations he had envisioned for his home. One such example, which he titled "Falling Leaves," was a series of twisted bamboo curtains hanging from the edges of the overhead trellis, redefining the space and modifying the light that entered into one of the courtyards. In this intervention could be seen Rose's inspiration to translate into landscape terms the "sense of transparency, and of visibility broken by a succession of planes" that was characteristic of the constructivist sculpture he admired. In the spring he wove cord between the ground and the overhead trellis to support the growth of vines in a way that referenced the woven chairs and combined with other materials to create rich, ambiguous spatial edges.[16] And he immediately recommenced his habit of using "found objects"—something he would regularly continue to do at Ridgewood, as elsewhere—transforming an old hibachi and a common hose nozzle into a pool and fountain.

Throughout the 1950s and 1960s Rose's home provided him with an island in the suburbs where he could experiment freely, irritating local authorities with his inventive counterpoint to the seemingly endless parade of equally set back ranch, cape, split level, and colonial houses that were rendering the rest of the suburban landscape as inadvertent, leftover space, festooned with foundation plantings, ornamental fruit trees, and useless front lawns. During this time Rose wrote prolifically (and was written about) in both popular garden magazines such as *House and Garden* and professional journals like *Progressive Architecture*. He published his first book, *Creative Gardens,* in 1958 and followed it up with the very different *Gardens Make Me Laugh* in 1965 and *Modern American Gardens—Designed by James Rose* in 1967; in *Modern American Gardens,* Rose (writing under the pseudonym Marc Snow) reflects on the changing essence of landscape design as he was experiencing it most intimately at his own home:

> The question of what happens to such landscapes in ten years or more is often raised. The answer is that they change. They change enormously with plant growth, with the change of attitudes and ideas of the people who live in them, with the unexpected and with the planned. With the revisions and alterations that come with growth, not just of plants but of the people as well. The trick is to devise an environment

"Falling Leaves," c. 1954. Courtesy JRC.

that will permit this growth—in fact, an environment that grows.[17]

At Ridgewood, as in his commissions of the 1950s and 1960s, Rose continued to experiment with the grid and modular landscapes, as well as with the free (obtuse-angled) form that would come to characterize his work, while conserving (and expressing) the character and natural features of his sites. He explored unconventional uses of common and recycled materials such as railroad ties, blacktop, fiberglass, and scrap metal, earning a reputation, through his inventive frugality, for having the "common touch." Among the scores of experimental modern residential gardens he designed were more examples of the house-and-garden. The Lois and Phillip Macht residence (1956) in Baltimore was one of these.

MACHT GARDEN
AND HOUSE

BALTIMORE, MARYLAND

(1956)

Phillip Macht was a young builder when he and his wife, Lois, sought to build their own home in 1955. They were determined to live in Mount Washington, an old neighborhood in Baltimore with very few undeveloped parcels of land available for new construction. The parcel they selected was almost unbuildable, a 1.25-acre lot on a busy street, heavily wooded with mature beech and oak on a steep (25 percent) northwest-facing slope. The Machts commissioned their older cousin, the New York architect Daniel "Duke" Schwartzman, to design their house, and he introduced them to Rose, with whom Schwartzman was working on a shopping center project in Europe at the time.[1]

Initially, Rose's role was to determine how to preserve trees while accommodating Schwartzman's design for a five-thousand-square-foot house that, to satisfy the Machts' program, would be limited to a single story. Soon, however, Schwartzman and the Machts parted ways, and, with

Schwartzman's blessing and the drafting assistance of the local architect Donald Radcliffe (who produced the necessary drawings for permits), Rose took over the project. For a landscape architect to design both house and landscape was certainly not common, but the Machts were sold on Rose and open to the possibilities of his landscape-based approach. For his part, Rose, who disapproved of Schwartzman's early house plans, wryly commented, "It was a happy experience.

Southeastern view of house terrace, 1957. Photograph by Ezra Stoller. © Ezra Stoller/Esto.

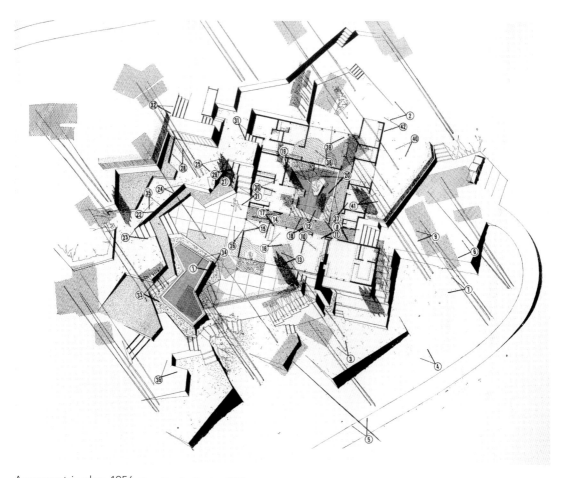

Axonometric plan, 1956. From *Creative Gardens* (1958).

The young couple were intelligent and cooperative and, on reflection, extremely appreciative at having been 'saved.'"[2]

Rose's basic idea was to develop the steeply sloping site into a series of terraces, tethered to existing trees and stitched together through a system of steps and paths. The largest of these terraces would include the house and would be "simply another level in the remade landscape."[3] Owing to the severity of the slope and the self-imposed discipline

West–east passageway, 1957. Photograph by Ezra Stoller. © Ezra Stoller/Esto.

of saving all the trees, the other terraces were by necessity relatively small, following the contours of the site as they wheeled around the large house-containing terrace. As Rose described his approach, "It should begin with the land, and the land should be sculpture—a bas relief creating level areas at the base of trees with the trees left undisturbed. I plotted all the trees on a contour map and studied the myriad possibilities for making levels—intervening, overlapping, projecting levels—with not disturbing trees as the basic discipline. I selected one level large enough to take the house, and an existing valley into which the pool could be tortured. The landscape problem, from then on, was a question of simplifying and integrating the various levels within a system of circulation."[4]

With the help of Macht's construction crew, all of the terraces were formed (with the exception of the pool) and even some of the planting was installed before the house slab

View from house toward eastern terrace, 1957. Photograph by Ezra Stoller. © Ezra Stoller / Esto.

was poured, revealing the edited relief of the landform in the woods. In *Creative Gardens,* Rose shares his pleasure at seeing the project during this phase of its construction: "At this stage, one got an unobstructed bird's-eye view from the alley above. The forms had begun to emerge, and it had the romantic quality of an ancient ruin. It had that particular vitality one finds at birth and death alike, and like that certain time of spring and fall which are almost indistinguishable. I knew if just *that* could be kept, it would be a fine house."[5]

View from interior playroom toward outdoor play space, 1957. Photograph by Ezra Stoller. © Ezra Stoller/Esto.

Rose divided his design for the largest terrace into three interrelated parts. The first included a passageway running west to east through the house from its entrance, three feet above the parking court at which one arrived. It connected to the master bedroom–study and opened to the living–dining space, as well as to on-grade outdoor spaces to its north and west through continuous fourteen-foot-high floor-to-ceiling glass. These outdoor spaces, in turn, opened to the other outdoor terraces above and below them. The second

Central atrium from west–east passageway, 1957. Photograph by Ezra Stoller. © Ezra Stoller/Esto.

East terraces, 1957. Photograph by Ezra Stoller. © Ezra Stoller/Esto.

part included a passageway running north–south through the house, connecting to three sleeping cubicles for children, with their own on-grade private garden to the east, as well as to a common playroom and—again through tall, continuous floor-to-ceiling glass—to an on-grade outdoor play space to the south. The children's outdoor play space, like the other outdoor spaces on this level, opened to more terraces above and beyond itself. The third part of this terrace included a kitchen and utility room, servant and guest rooms, and a delivery entrance on the southwest side. Here the house and large terrace ended together, with a simple doorway leading to a series of small terraces and steps to the service alley above. All the outdoor terraces were connected by paths and contained within buffer plantings, mostly of hemlock, along the site's borders. At the center of Rose's tripartite scheme was an atrium that, as he describes it, "brings with it a sense of the landscape continuing through the house, and the interior passageways, bordering the atrium on two sides, directly communicate with the outdoors."[6]

Rose designed his angular "bas relief" using railroad tie walls and risers, adding plants where needed to provide privacy and to further define edges. On the surfaces closest to the indoor dining and living spaces he continued the grid of the house with eight-foot squares of exposed aggregate concrete, paving a large asphalt trapezoid around an existing mature oak. Common and often recycled materials—such as wood chips, gravel, granite setts (reclaimed from Baltimore streets), and more asphalt—as well as stones found on-site made up the rest of the ground planes of the outdoor terraces and steps. Of Rose's unconventional use of asphalt around the base of trees, as treads, and on the terraces, Lois Macht recalls,

> He convinced us easily that blacktop was the ultimate material because if you did it right it was permeable and so water didn't accumulate on the top and you had a covering which kept the weeds down and made it useful. He had a definite formula for the blacktop, by the way, and he had to argue with everybody about how to do it right. Once though we had a charitable luncheon here. It was a hot day and the ladies were in very high heels and the heels went into the blacktop

and tracked it everywhere. That was when we decided to remove the blacktop close to the house.[7]

Having established the terraces and framed the house and its spaces, it became necessary to design the details of the interior of the building. Inverting the normal process, Rose called on the architect Henry Hebbeln, a collaborator for whose houses Rose sometimes designed landscapes. As Lois Macht remembers, "The basic framework of this house was Jim's, but then we said, but you know we have to eat! We need a kitchen and kitchen cabinets. And Jim said, 'Oh, well I have a good friend who's a wonderful architect and he has 'impeccable taste,' which was of course a real insult in Jim's eyes. Using old railroad ties [and blacktop!] doesn't exactly jibe with impeccable taste!'"[8]

For almost a year Rose and Hebbeln were on-site virtually every week, working out details of the house with the Machts and conspiring to eliminate any separation between inside and out. Elements such as the indoor–outdoor trellis piercing the glass wall and floating above an interior brazier, as well as the egg-crate ceiling treatment over the passageways, were designed to emphasize the fluency of the space. Hebbeln was an excellent designer and was easy to get along with, while Rose's quick wit and biting sense of humor sometimes alienated both clients and crews, as he frequently, and often sardonically, insisted that things be redone. Still, Rose is remembered by Lois Macht with great respect and affection; as she thoughtfully described his demeanor in an interview fifty-five years later, "He had a long thin face . . . a very intense look . . . but a wonderful smile, BIG smile . . . and when he smiled, that's when you knew he was the devil."[9]

As he did with several other projects, Rose meticulously documented the Macht residence in *Creative Gardens,* with

Interior brazier and north terrace, 1957. Photograph by Ezra Stoller. © Ezra Stoller/Esto.

another illustrative plan by Charles Rieger keyed to over forty images by Ezra Stoller and Lonnie Wasco. In 1960 the project was published by *Progressive Architecture* in "Houses and Landscapes," an interesting article the magazine cooked up in which Rose, Lawrence Halprin, and Karl Linn critiqued one another's work. While neither Halprin nor Linn had visited the Macht site, both criticized Rose's "incessant" and unsystematic angular terraces. (Rose, of course, was highly critical of their projects as well.) Eight months later the Macht residence was awarded the annual *House and Garden* "Hallmark" award for the best residential design in the country, with Rose's creation being praised for its harmonious fusion of house and garden, such that "it is hard to tell where one begins and the other ends."[10]

Today many changes to this almost sixty-year-old landscape are readily apparent. The outdoor parts of the large terrace have been altered, sometimes with strangely out of place curving forms, and have been repaved with brick or decking. On the periphery the forest has filled in some of the terraced spaces. Many of Rose's original plantings did not survive in the heavy soils. Here and there timbers have rotted out and need replacing. But ample evidence of Rose's "bas relief" remains, along with its rich unconventional textures and patterns made of common (if unexpected) or recycled materials. Some of these materials—such as his specially formulated blacktop, now complemented here and there with bright green moss—have become even more intriguing. Most significant, the integrated indoor–outdoor space is still there, flowing in these woods almost freely through an almost transparent house-and-garden.

AVERETT GARDEN
AND HOUSE

COLUMBUS, GEORGIA

(1959)

In 1958, Mary Keith Averett and her husband, Clifford, purchased and subdivided some wooded land in Columbus, Georgia, selecting for themselves the choicest hilltop lot, characterized by moderate to steep slopes and longleaf and loblolly pine, as well as water oak, southern red oak, and sweetgum. They hired Rozier Dedwylder, a local architect and family friend, to design their house. Dedwylder in turn provided Mary Keith with several books on landscape design, including Rose's recently published *Creative Gardens*. As Mrs. Averett recalled, "The architect gave me several landscape books to look over, and I just stayed awake all night looking at Jim's first book. I called to see if he would recommend anyone in the area and he said he would come himself."[1]

When Rose arrived in Georgia (as the tale goes, wearing different colored socks), a symmetrical, two-story colonial house had already been designed.[2] Meeting with Mrs. Averett at the site, he proceeded to cut up the architectural

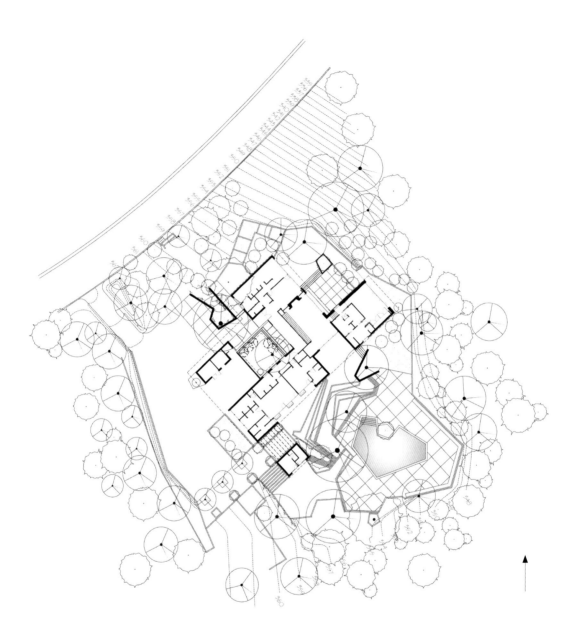

Plan, 2014. Drawn by Shanshan Yu. Courtesy JRC.

plans with scissors, reorienting and reorganizing the interior spaces to respond to the site's topography, vegetation, and views. When he was done, the two-story house was reconceived as a single-story dwelling divided into a series of three interior levels (terraces) based on the site's topography. These levels flowed through walls of glass onto more levels (terraces) outside, thus enabling a sense of continuity between the house, the garden, and the wooded landscape and setting the stage for the detailed design of an integral modern house-and-garden that could embrace the character of the place, incorporating existing site features such as the mature trees that were present on the lot. As Mrs. Averett recalled, "I had been told a steep lot such as mine could produce an outstanding house, but didn't have a clue how that would happen until Jim."[3] Well after construction was complete, Rose summarized the design:

> Inner spaces communicate with outer. The link is the levels, handled rhythmically, fluidly, with no separation. Seen from the house the levels flow into a pool platform in the woods. From the pool, the inner recesses of the house communicate in a different way through the same handling of levels. Outside, a series of levels brings the viewer into a network of spaces—architectural, natural, divided and connected—varying in size, proportion, direction, purpose and materials, but always a thing of which the viewer is inevitably a part.[4]

The highest level of the site supported entering and parking, incorporating existing trees on its edges. To the northeast, visitors' parking was partly defined by a raised concrete sidewalk that was embedded with locally sourced brownish pebble aggregate. (These pebbles were used throughout the site, including on paths and on the roof of the house.) Behind the gridded sidewalk, an irregular, sitting-height retaining wall of native fieldstone, similar in color to the pebbles and matching the fieldstone veneer of the adjacent garage and house, further defined the space and maintained the grades around existing mature trees; its angled form led the eye toward the entrance to the

Approach to house entry from parking area, 1962. Photograph by William Barksdale. Courtesy Sidney and Rebecca Yarbrough.

house. From here one descended over two long, shallow steps that extended the length of a perfectly square, sunken entry court designed around an existing mature loblolly pine and edged on the other three sides by the house and garage. Along these L-shaped steps, Rose added a veil of five loquat trees, closely planted on a grid.

One entered the house at its highest level, through a wooden door in the otherwise transparent northeastern

Entry courtyard, 1962. Photograph by William Barksdale. Courtesy Sidney and Rebecca Yarbrough.

View from living room toward entry court, 1962. Photograph by William Barksdale. Courtesy Sidney and Rebecca Yarbrough.

wall. A long interior hallway ran beside the tree-veiled out-door court and overlooked the main living room below, connected to it physically by four protracted stairs. At one end of the hall the kitchen and dining rooms looked out through floor-to-ceiling glass over the wooded landscape to the northeast, while the den, a guest room, and a suite of bedrooms were at the hall's other end. These latter rooms opened visually and physically to Rose's elongated, irregular railroad tie and asphalt terrace steps, which were punctuated by existing trees and which descended to the "pool plat-form" within the surrounding woods.

The second interior level was occupied by the main living room, a large space (thirty by twenty feet) with an eighteen-foot-high gabled ceiling. It was perforated on three sides with glass walls connecting to the outdoors and had a stone fireplace wall on its fourth side. Above the long stairs to the southwest was the entry court. On the opposite side of the

View from guest room looking south, 1962. Photograph by William Barksdale. Courtesy Sidney and Rebecca Yarbrough.

living room was an almost on-grade outdoor terrace in the woods. In between, the space opened through a glass door within a pentagon of floor-to-ceiling glazing to a small lanai, defined by extensions of the indoor living room's gabled ceiling and floor planes as well as by the fieldstone-clad exterior wall folding inward through the glass to edge the living room, as it did the lanai. Looking through the glass pentagon, immediately at the far edge of the lanai, one could see a great longleaf pine against the forest background, the tree's beautifully textured vertical trunk wrapped in a low, irregular, horizontal fieldstone retaining wall that began to lead one's eye (to be followed by one's feet) outward, along the jagged railroad ties, over the rough asphalt terrace steps, under the canopy of retained trees, and toward the designed oasis that Rose surgically cut and filled into the forest below.

This oasis was the heart of the Averett residence's landscape design. Flowing from the interior living spaces, edged by Rose's irregular, elongated, tree-containing steps and the gabled, stone-clad house to the northwest, the garden projected asymmetrically into the forest on its other three sides, which were defined by a broad, angled bench; a secondary entrance spilled in from the parking area above. Twisted within the space, an obtuse-angled swimming pool was interlocked with a gridded, exposed aggregate concrete ground plane, recalling the front entry and forming a kind of yin/yang relationship between land and water, a single, somewhat picturesque cotoneaster punctuating their nexus.[5] The space was bathed with dappled light along its edges as the sun wheeled around, and it had the feeling of a woodland glade, even though it was made, in large measure, of recycled railroad ties, asphalt, and concrete, reminding us of Rose's admonition that, as a spatial experience, a garden can be made of anything.

Living room, lanai, and landscape, 1962. Photograph by William Barksdale. Courtesy Sidney and Rebecca Yarbrough.

View from lanai to pool, 1962. Photograph by William Barksdale. Courtesy Sidney and Rebecca Yarbrough.

Multi-gabled roof and irregular terraces compose the space, 1962. Photograph by William Barksdale. Courtesy Sidney and Rebecca Yarbrough.

The third and lowest level within the house connected the inside living room with the master suite to its northeast via several steps descending through a narrow passage. Like other interior spaces, the master bedroom flowed through floor-to-ceiling glass to a private outdoor terrace that, like all the outdoor spaces, was interconnected with the rest of the garden levels through paths around the house. Whether inside or out, one moved within this landscape as Rose had intended, experiencing from a shifting, kaleidoscopic view-point this "thing of which the viewer is inevitably a part" and sensing one's connection with the infinite through the natural features of the site.[6]

In 1974 the Averetts sold their home to Sidney and Rebecca Yarbrough, but Mary Keith Averett clearly appreciated the creative force at work in her environment while she lived there. As she reflected on revisiting it in 2005, "It's a work of art that I'm proud to have been associated with. . . . It was truly an embellishment of a wonderful natural site."[7] For over forty years, the Yarbroughs have been the home's stewards, and they remain inspired by the groundwork laid by Rose, Mary Keith Averett, and Dedwylder. As Rebecca Yarbrough has remarked, "Every room you walk into brings nature into you and you feel a part of the whole picture. . . . To me this home has a spirit that lives and is here for you

Mary Keith Averett on master suite terrace, 1962. Photograph by William Barksdale. Courtesy Sidney and Rebecca Yarbrough.

Pool and terraces, 2014. Photograph by author. Courtesy JRC.

to partake of."[8] Making only minor changes over the years, the Yarbroughs have faithfully replaced and rebuilt much of the landscape and architectural design as it has aged during their occupancy. Sidney Yarbrough will authoritatively tell you how many railroad ties can be cut before resharpening your chainsaw blade. Notwithstanding some settlement of concrete, a few minor alterations, and the loss of some plants, the Averett design remains in fine condition today, thanks in large measure to the Yarbroughs' exceptional sensitivity and care.

G-V Controls courtyard, view from roof, mid-1960s. Courtesy JRC.

G-V CONTROLS
COURTYARD

LIVINGSTON, NEW JERSEY
(1960)

The relationship between sculpture and landscape inspired Rose's thinking and writing from the outset of his career. In the tiny (forty-four by sixty-six feet) courtyard at G-V Controls, a new suburban electronics assembly factory and office building in Livingston, New Jersey, Rose created his own abstract modern sculptures, in the forms of scrap metal lanterns and a fountain, as integral parts of a larger "space-sculpture" one moved through.[1] Certainly by 1960 the reuse of scavenged "scraps" to make gardens was not new to Rose, but his recycling of leftover copper sheeting and brass tubing found in a junk heap at this electronics plant was the first time he experimented with such materials, and it would inspire the design and integration of many subsequent scrap metal sculptures in future gardens.

Designed in a U-shape around a central courtyard by the architectural firm Frank Grad and Sons, the G-V Controls building was constructed in 1959 by William L.

Blanchard and Company. Rose designed the courtyard for G-V president Charles Gear in 1960, the year Rose went to Japan to participate in the World Design Conference. Intended to be used for contemplation and to be experienced from office windows, this courtyard suggested a modern American expression of the Zen gardens that so intrigued Rose and with which he was beginning to become more intimately familiar. In the "cap-

Scrap metal lanterns illuminate fountain and landscape, 1963. Photograph by David Hirsch. Courtesy JRC.

Reflection of garden forms in pool. From *Modern American Gardens* (1967).

tion story" that Rose wrote to accompany photographs of the courtyard in *Modern American Gardens,* one can also detect a metaphysical expression of Rose's transcendentalist beliefs—even a growing mysticism—as Rose visualizes the universe in the small, abstract details reflected in the courtyard pool:

> To see the universe within a place
> is to see a garden;
> to see it so
> is to have a garden;
> not to prevent its happening
> is to build a garden.[2]

While certainly related to many things Rose was thinking and experiencing, this small project remains

Abstract ground plane elements. From *Modern American Gardens.*

best defined as a modern American garden (or, more precisely, courtyard) designed by James Rose—a tiny, abstract, asymmetrical, physical, continuous-though-interrupted, guided space-experience made of common materials and re-formed scraps and meant to evoke the metaphysical fusion of a modern individual with the infinite. Using ordinary things like pebbles, wood planks, water, hose nozzles, honey locusts, birches, yews, and ground cover, along with his refashioned scrap metal sculptures, Rose divided the tiny space into an always-changing cosmic experience, noting,

> As the participant moves, the garden moves,
> and each is involved in an infinity
> of relationships wherein the sky,
> the earth, the man—and the handiwork of each—

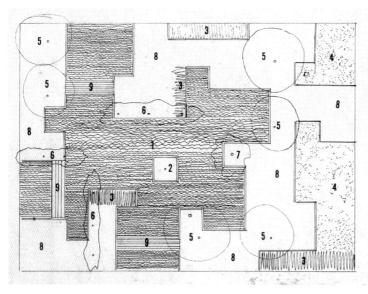

IDYL IN AN ELECTRONICS FACTORY

The asymmetrical but formally balanced design for the garden can be deduced by studying the plan. Designer Rose balanced each visual force with a counterforce, each visual weight with a counterweight. The factory employee who looks out from his desk senses none of this, but rather a poetic vision of nature. If heaven were small, it might look like this.

key to plan

1 pool
2 fountain island
3 low hedge
4 ground cover
5 honey locust trees
6 white birch trees
7 weeping yew tree
8 pebbles
9 wood bridge

Plan, 1963. From *Interiors* (July 1963).

become one.[3]

The courtyard's surface was distributed modularly, almost equally, between a shallow reflecting pool of dark water and a ground plane of light-colored gravel. The three-sided space was divided by plantings, organized into three rows of birches, six locusts, three short sections of yew hedge, and one specimen weeping yew, with ground cover along the courtyard's open edge. Three wooden planks bridged the graveled land over the water, while on an island near the center of the pool, Rose's twelve-foot-high abstract scrap metal fountain, meant to evoke a family of growing plants, emerged. This assemblage of scrap metal was conceived not as a separate sculptural object but as a fully integrated part of the garden experience, dividing space and contributing to interspatial vistas as one moved through the courtyard. As Rose saw it,

> . . . and the fountain is not a thing apart—
> made or placed in isolation to the rest.
> It is sheets of copper and tubes of brass
> wrought as forms-in-space that guide the water
> for a while and let it go again
> as the birches and the locusts hold the spaces
> between them—and yet do not—
> and the sunlight visits like a proper guest
> at just the moment that the water sparkles and the
> pebbles show
> and then it goes—and comes again.[4]

Rose used the same leftover "sheets of copper" to make abstract lanterns, which he intended to be equally integral to the design. He understood the scraps he used to make the lanterns for their inherent qualities and abstract charac-

Scrap metal fountain, 1963. Photograph by David Hirsch. From *Interiors* (July 1963).

teristics which he could manipulate and re-form into "lanterns" to fuse with other materials and the integral space. He describes one such lantern as

> the same copper sheeting
> that twisted into shapes
> at night, or twisted night itself,
> or let itself be twisted
> and then came back to day.[5]

Unfortunately, the courtyard, its scrap metal sculptures, and the G-V Controls building no longer exist, except in the record Rose left on the front cover and at the beginning of *Modern American Gardens,* where his illustrated "cap-

"Snake dance" variation, James Rose Center, mid-1970s. Courtesy JRC.

Lantern-mask, 1970s. Courtesy JRC.

tion story" of the courtyard is juxtaposed with Marc Snow's "insightful" description of Rose's methods and Snow's narrative history of landscape architecture's modern movement. Despite its loss, the project's significance endured, inspiring Rose to experiment with designing other scrap metal fountains and lanterns in future gardens. One such work was the mobile "snake dance" fountain Rose designed for a German *Gartenbauausstellung* in Hamburg just shortly after completing G-V Controls, which in turn served as the inspiration for numerous serpent fountains integrated into Rose's home in Ridgewood and elsewhere.

Rose with "snake dance" fountain, early 1960s. Courtesy JRC.

Another example of how his experience at G-V Controls inspired Rose was a scrap metal lantern that he formed into a perforated abstract mask by cutting and folding some flat, leftover copper roof flashing into three dimensions, not entirely unlike the way in which paper is cut and folded in origami. At Ridgewood, a similar lantern-mask was perched on a stand made from the trunk of a dead hemlock, at night sending light into space through its angular features and illuminating, along with itself, other parts of Rose's larger, evolving garden intervention—a sculpture within a sculpture. In ways such as this Rose continued to adjust his design for his home during its first fifteen years, but in 1968 he embarked on major changes that would utterly transform it.

Buddha Garden, Rose garden and house, early 1970s. Courtesy JRC.

ROSE GARDEN AND HOUSE

RIDGEWOOD, NEW JERSEY

(PART 2: 1968–1991)

In June 1967 Rose and his mother took out a $24,000 loan to support major alterations to their home which were necessitated by changing circumstances in their lives and by the home's evolving function as a study center for Zen and the martial arts (including, most particularly, landscape design, which Rose had come to understand as one).[1] By the end of 1968 these renovations were complete. With significant changes to shelters and landscape, Rose's by now characteristic obtuse-angled spatial geometry, only hinted at in the original ground patterns of two of the 1953 courtyards, had emerged throughout, as it had done in his commissioned projects. The resulting metamorphosis of form was not only a response to the angled eastern property line but also a reflection of Rose's preference for freer, angular, sequenced "space-form" to provoke a modern Western transcendental experience.

Rose increased the sheltered portions of his design. Kitchens were added to both his and Jean's studios, making each studio self-sufficient. Minnie's and Jean's separate sheltered spaces were merged, allowing Jean easier access to her aging mother, and much of what had been Minnie's bedroom garden was converted into a fully enclosed interior courtyard in the process. The original glass walls were bumped out almost everywhere, and four wooden platforms were added in the newly captured sheltered spaces, providing interior perches on which to sit, eat, or meditate. Three of these platforms hovered just above adjacent garden spaces, essentially allowing for occupation of the edge between inside and out. In recognition of his mobile lifestyle, and in anticipation of renting out his studio, Rose expanded his interior living space twelve feet to the south, and the glass wall that had conjoined the space with the adjacent courtyard was replaced by an opaque masonry one. This not only increased the studio's interior living space and degree of privacy but also visually focused the new interior volume on the evolving garden to its east.

Masonry wall encloses addition to northern shelter, 1998. Photograph by author. Courtesy JRC.

Expansion of central shelter eastward, early 1970s. Photograph by Don Manza. Courtesy JRC.

A two-car gravel parking area was incised adjacent to the studio along Southern Parkway, further supporting the studio's rentability. Since the white pines Rose had planted for privacy had grown, shading out their own lower branches, delicately woven wooden fences (probably inspired, like his woven plastic cord chairs and benches, by Jean's and Minnie's weaving) were constructed along Ridgewood Avenue and Southern Parkway for additional screening.[2] The original kitchen court between Minnie's shelter and Southern Parkway was expanded, and the vegetable garden was converted to outdoor storage. A garden pool and planter replaced the lawn in the relatively large eastern terrace, adjusting and

New parking space off Southern Parkway, early 1970s. Photograph by Don Manza. Courtesy JRC.

making sculptural and spatial what was essentially a two-dimensional ground pattern in the original grid. Additional plantings of dogwoods, cherries, and rhododendrons also contributed to the transformation of the space, increasing privacy and redefining the canopy.

These renovations reflected the family's efforts to adjust their environment to changing circumstances, as well as Rose's evolving aesthetic point of view. Sadly, in 1969, not long after the renovations were completed, Minnie died. In the following years Rose continued his pattern of designing, writing, traveling, and improvising at Ridgewood.[3] Besides the metal lanterns and snake fountains he was continually moving around, Rose's improvisations included an angled screen he constructed along a small segment of the eastern edge of the property to provide more enclosure and privacy as Ridgewood Avenue became busier. Made of upended split rails from a salvaged post and rail fence, the improvisation got him into trouble with Ridgewood's building inspector. Informed that it was illegal to have a fence higher than four feet on one's property line (which, of course, he knew), Rose defiantly exclaimed, "That is not a fence—it is a pole arrangement!"[4] The building inspector took him to court, and of course the judge agreed that it was not a "pole arrangement" but a fence and ordered Rose to take it down. Yet years later the "pole arrangement" remained at the site.

"Pole arrangement," late 1970s. Courtesy JRC.

Woven fences and new entrance, northern garden, 1982. Photograph by Alan Ward.

A few weeks before his death in 1991, Rose reflected, "You know, Dean, my whole life people have said to me, 'you can't do it, you can't do it, you can't do it.'" He then raised a trembling finger to point at his "pole arrangement," visible through the glass wall between his bed and the garden, and defiantly exclaimed, "There it is!"[5]

In the early 1970s Rose began constructing a roof garden to get still more living space from his "half a tennis

Pool and "rock ikebana," eastern courtyard, 1982. Photograph by Alan Ward.

court," an idea that he had had in mind from the beginning. Reflecting his practice of Zen Buddhism and his desire to use his home as a center for martial arts, the first stage of the roof garden contained a zendo (a room for meditation and retreat). It was surrounded by a peripheral walkway and gallery punctured from below by the branches of one of the site's original ailanthus trees. Alongside the zendo he constructed an outdoor apartment (complete with fireplace)

Zendo, early 1980s. Courtesy JRC.

intended for visiting monks and, adjacent to that, a gathering space over the original communal space of his mother's shelter. Access to the roof garden from the shelter below was provided by a new stairway, with one side built against the southern storage wall of the now-interior courtyard that had once been Minnie's bedroom garden, and the other supported by an overhead beam stitched to the treads with metal cables.[6] Outdoor access to the surrounding walkway from the renovated eastern garden space was provided by a spiral staircase located outside the northeast corner of the newly defined interior space.

The zendo provided Rose with a place to hold group

meditation sessions, consistent with his home's evolving function as a Zen retreat. His own morning meditations in the zendo helped Rose to become the "clear channel" he wanted to be when spontaneously designing and building gardens without preconceptions. While such methods were undoubtedly encouraged by his exposure to Japan and Zen Buddhism, they were also consistent with Rose's assertion that landscape design should not be preconceived, a viewpoint he had expressed decades earlier in opposing the Beaux-Arts system at Harvard.

The new gathering space adjacent to the outdoor apartment on the roof became defined in large part by a folded,

Roof garden looking south, mid-1970s. Photograph by Don Manza. Courtesy JRC.

Bridge to northern roof garden, mid-1970s. Courtesy JRC.

angled roof-wall. Its leaflike structural framework was alternately sheathed with opaque or translucent materials (opalescent fiberglass) or left completely open to the interpenetrating trees, sky, and light. Described by Rose in *The Heavenly Environment* as a "pattern of organic (rather than cosmetic) decoration and an integral division of space," the resulting space was at once clearly expressed yet delightfully ambiguous, defying classification even of space and edge, along with shelter and landscape.[7] Here one could perhaps most clearly experience what Rose meant when he described his home as being neither indoors nor out, but both.

By 1974 other changes to the design included the addition of a bathroom to the northeast of the conjoined shelters and of planting areas to the east of the original studio, now often rented. The second stage of the roof garden was completed as well. It included a bridge over the space between the now two shelters, allowing expansion of the roof garden spaces to include a new garden space over the studio. The edges of this space were created by angled planter boxes that served as seats and by other structures sheathed with opalescent fiberglass that clearly recalled Rose's 1940s and 1950s designs for modular gardens, as well as by the branches and needles of the maturing white pines originally planted to screen and define the ground space below.

Northern courtyard beneath bridge, mid-1970s. Photograph by Don Manza. Courtesy JRC.

Near the northern end of the bridge Rose incorporated another spiral stairway, which provided a second outdoor connection between the roof garden and the garden on the ground while also serving as a post support for the bridge. After the addition of a second bridge connecting back to a new roof garden over Minnie's original kitchen, work on the roof garden was essentially finished. A continuous three-dimensional loop incorporating upstairs and down,

Western courtyard, 1982. Photograph by Alan Ward.

as well as inside and out, had been completed, as Rose fully utilized his entire site, including the roofs of the shelters, for living.

Between 1974 and 1976 shoji screens were added to the glass walls throughout the assemblage. By 1982 all the planters in the eastern portion of the site had been converted into reflecting pools, with fountains made from hose nozzles attached to submersible pumps plugged into extension cords. Terraces and pools were repaved using large, angular Pennsylvania bluestone slabs, with occasional groupings of round river stones interspersed among tree roots that also became part of the ground pattern as they grew. The gravel parking area added in 1968 was paved with the same river stones surrounded by broken bluestone fragments. "Rock ikebana," as Rose referred to the sculptural arrangements of found rocks he was incorporating into some of his gardens, were placed among the other stones and plants, many of which were volunteers that he allowed to remain.[8]

The rest of the 1980s saw fewer inventive changes to the space. The southern spiral staircase and the last of the two bridges Rose constructed were removed. The remaining bridge was rebuilt, and handrails were added after a prospective client fell to the ground, breaking her neck.[9] (She still hired Rose.) Things continued to shift and be shifted, but in the last decade before Rose died, his inventive counterpoint to the typical suburban home, designed to change and to be redesigned continuously, quickly and profoundly began to deteriorate.

Native rocks rearranged, Paley garden, 1970s. Courtesy JRC.

PALEY GARDEN

SADDLE RIVER, NEW JERSEY

(1974)

In 1973 the architect Eleanore Pettersen introduced Rose to Florence and Edward Paley, for whom Pettersen was designing a house on a very rocky landscape in Saddle River, New Jersey. The two-acre site sloped downward to the northwest and was covered by a mature woodland of oaks and other hardwoods. Rose described the clients as having an uncommon respect for the existing forest:

> In our first walking of the site, the Paleys showed an intense interest in the natural cover—the moss and the ground pine, as well as existing trees, including a few apple trees which looked abandoned in an otherwise woodland setting. There is nothing so unusual about an interest in the natural growth; many clients have intense interest in their ownership, but when it comes to touch and go—a question of what to sacrifice for what—the "intense interest" in moss and

ground pine often turns out to be a rather sentimental attachment. Not so with the Paleys.[1]

Together Rose and Florence Paley made sure the natural cover would be relatively undisturbed during construction of the house, thus maintaining the character of the woodland and allowing for the incorporation of existing vegetation into the fabric of the space.[2] Rose converted the construction road they had carefully incised through the forest into an entry drive with several adjacent parking niches, using railroad ties as edging and planting an understory of native rhododendrons and hemlocks to further define the angular, linear space. The

Entry drive, 1994. Photograph by R. Hruby. Courtesy JRC.

Entry court, looking from house to entry drive, 1994. Photograph by R. Hruby. Courtesy JRC.

drive resolved in a generous entry court edged on two sides by a low railroad-tie retaining wall that defined the space and maintained the grades of existing trees. As he had done along the drive, Rose planted more native broad-leaved evergreens above the retaining wall to its north and east, further enclosing the space. South of the court and adjacent to the front door, broad, shallow irregular steps and an apple tree that had been saved helped to define the threshold between the parking court and the interior foyer. A line of three large and closely

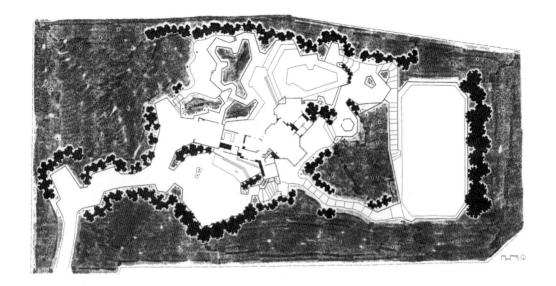

Figure-ground diagram, 1994. Drawn by R. Hruby. Courtesy JRC.

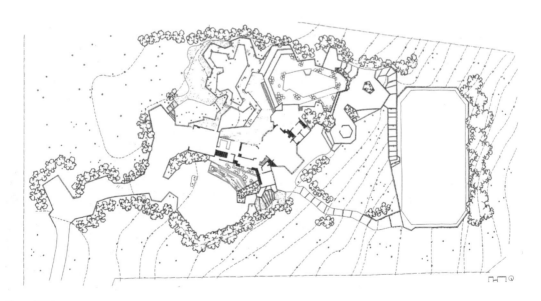

Plan, 1994. Drawn by R. Hruby. Courtesy JRC.

spaced mature oaks was retained within the court, dividing the space somewhat asymmetrically. A spur of road off the main trajectory of the drive led to the garage and service area.

The main section of the house ran roughly east–west, parallel to the contours of the land, with a southeastern wing culminating in the garage, forming an open L-shape that began to define an outdoor space to the south. On entering the house from the parking court, one was directed to the great living room, a large space that overlooked the forest descending to the north and opened through floor-to-ceiling glass walls and doors to an angular segmented walk within the existing woods to the south. A long, irregular three-sided deck connected the indoor living space to this meandering walk, as well as to a lower pool-containing terrace, providing ample room to sit and overlook either space.

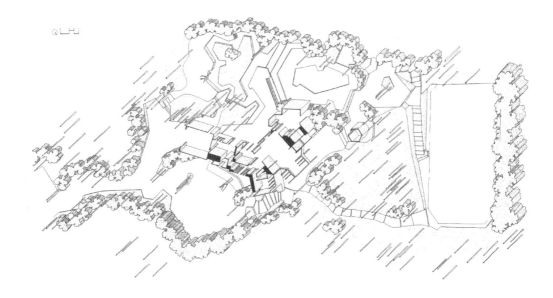

Axonometric plan, 1994. Drawn by R. Hruby. Courtesy JRC.

From the deck or the woodland walk one could move directly to the pool terrace over several broad and long tie-and-asphalt steps. Here Rose's characteristic angular pool was punctuated by various sculptures (not created by Rose). From the pool terrace one moved over a series of more constrained steps and landings to additional terraces running along the northern edge of the house; these terraces connected to a "walk-out" basement before returning to the entry court above. At the ends of these lower terraces, paths on either side of the house descended about ten more feet through the forest to a tennis court.

At the Paley site, Rose incorporated existing trees and

Rear deck and asphalt and timber steps, c. 1991. Courtesy JRC.

subtly terraced the north-sloping landform with railroad-tie stairs and walls to redefine the experience of the woodland. The site's extensive glacial deposits offered him the unique opportunity to reveal the underlying geology by translating the plethora of subsurface stones into paths and other surfaces throughout the garden, as well as arranging them into what he called "rock ikebana." These abstract, often figural assemblages of large to medium-sized found stones or boulders had begun to have increasing expression in other of Rose's gardens, including his own home. In one such arrangement Rose appeared to capture the essence of his client, Florence Paley, whom he later recast as Medea in *The*

Pool terrace, c. 1991. Courtesy JRC.

Heavenly Environment, his last book.[3] Reflecting on the experience of discovering the accumulation of stones that had been unearthed—and then, to his surprise, reburied—by the backhoe operator during construction, Rose writes,

> I, for one, can never view stones as something dead—or "non-living," as the jargon goes—any more than I can view the good earth as so much "dirt." I know people who do just that, and they never cease to amaze me because it seems like a "back-up-the-wagon-and-get-rid-of-the-trash" view of life without ever having bothered to examine what someone else had decided was "trash."

Lower terrace between pool and tennis courts, 1994. Photograph by R. Hruby. Courtesy JRC.

"Rock ikebana," 1970s. Courtesy JRC.

In looking for essence or character, I feel more inclined to examine the garbage pail than the dinner menu, and in that sense the accumulating stones on the Paley job began to intrigue me.[4]

Rose had discussed the use of stones in gardens for decades, but in 1986 he clarified his attitude toward using the ones he found on his sites (as well as his general attitude toward conventional practices), stating simply but pointedly: "I don't bring in rocks to look at them or talk to them, but rocks that are on the site I try to use, instead of digging a hole to bury them, as if they were something obscene."[5]

By the time of the Paley job Rose had forged an exclusive arrangement with his own personally trained crew, led by foreman Rui Barardo, whose company Rose named Entourage. Working constantly with Rui and others, including the father-and-son masons Henry and Mike Ruepp (who also frequently worked on Pettersen's houses), enabled Rose to exercise greater control with his spontaneous on-site design-build method as it evolved in the 1970s and 1980s. With their assistance, "junk stones" found on rocky sites, not unlike railroad ties or scrap metal, began to serve Rose's "greater purpose" in the garden, helping to create that guiding spatial framework within which his modern clients and their guests could better perceive their relation to nature.

The Paley garden no longer exists, destroyed by subsequent development. However, a record of Rose's spontaneous intervention at the site can be found in photographs and in hand-drawn "plans" made in 1992–1993 as part of the James Rose Garden Documentation Project.[6]

ANISFIELD GARDEN

SADDLE RIVER, NEW JERSEY

(1983)

As with the Paleys, Rose was introduced to Richard and Millicent Anisfield by the architect Eleanore Pettersen, who had been hired by the couple to design a home for a three-acre site in Saddle River, New Jersey. Pettersen's modern spatial sense and respect for the existing conditions of the site provided Rose with interior spaces intended to relate to the outdoors, as well as a relatively unspoiled terrain that his intervention could interpret. Built without plans in 1982–1983, the garden remained undocumented until 1994 and, like most of Rose's work from the 1970s and 1980s, is still generally unknown, even though it is one of his most thorough integrations of site, architecture, and landscape.[1]

Once part of a farm enclosed by eight-foot-wide stone walls, when construction of the Anisfield residence began in 1982, the heavily wooded site gradually sloped downward from the street on its north side at a grade of about 3 percent. Rose carefully regraded the slope into interlocking terraces,

Figure-ground diagram, 1994. Drawn by R. Hruby. Courtesy JRC.

Plan, 1994. Drawn by R. Hruby. Courtesy JRC.

Axonometric plan, 1994. Drawn by R. Hruby. Courtesy JRC.

his characteristic obtuse-angled earthen "bas relief" subtle enough not to disturb the roots of existing trees but clear enough to begin to define new spaces in the woods. The ancient river stones just beneath the surface began to reveal themselves during excavation, and as the earlier farmers had done, Rose put the stones to work, using them to make walls as well as to edge the drive and paths, define slopes and ground surfaces, and make "rock ikebana" and stone lanterns that articulated key moments in the spatial sequence.

The entrance to the site was marked by one such expression: a stone lantern, made from a boulder Rose uncovered there, together with some leftover shards of Pennsylvania bluestone that Rose used for paving, all set on a surface of carefully embedded, cobble-sized rounded stones from the site. By the early 1980s, it had become common for Rose to forego his special mix of asphalt or gridded, exposed aggregate concrete in favor of skillfully executed surface compositions of white pebbles, cobbles (or other stones found on sites), and large angular slabs of bluestone mined in the northeastern part of Pennsylvania (not far from Rose's birthplace in Matamoras). In these surfaces one saw careful, inventive stonework, similar to that of many Japanese gardens.

Entering the property, one descended beneath the canopy along a curving driveway pressed slightly into the earth. On small slopes edging the drive, Rose's scavenged glacial river stones were carefully embedded in a manner reminiscent of the meticulous setting of river stones along the banks of bodies of water in some Japanese gardens, such as those at Katsura Imperial Villa and Nijo Castle in Kyoto. Rose planted native rhododendrons in the understory behind these slopes to help further define the drive and to screen out the public street.

As one approached the parking court, the canopy began to open a bit, allowing more light to enter the space. Here the native stone embankments edging the driveway resolved into three- to four-foot-high dry-laid stone retaining walls, some of which were terraced, edging the parking court. Rose planted more native rhododendrons in the understory behind these walls, further defining the space; these broad-leaved evergreens also helped to screen the street and create privacy as they directed one's attention toward the front door of the house. Two large maples were preserved within the court, dividing it somewhat and evoking a sense of integration with the forest. No ordinary parking area, this entry court was the terminus of a carefully choreographed spatial sequence. On stepping out of the car into this well-defined space, one was already in the garden.

Lantern at site entrance, 2014. Photograph by author. Courtesy JRC.

Entry court, 1994. Photograph by R. Hruby. Courtesy JRC.

To enter the house, one descended a series of irregu-lar bluestone steps that were constructed by Mike Ruepp, who, like foreman Rui Barrado, had been working closely with Rose for almost fifteen years.[2] Two more maples interrupted the stairs, as they led to a small bluestone land-ing with a narrow stream on either side that both managed and celebrated the movement of water from the roof and landscape. Together with the floor of the interior living spaces and a large rear deck, this landing occupied a sin-gle level, roughly three feet below the parking court. At the end of the landing, in the shade of the overhanging roof, Pettersen's dark, deeply carved wooden door marked a cavelike gateway: the entrance to the "sheltered part" of the woodland garden.

The house was a splayed U-shape with a massive stone chimney separating the entry foyer from the trapezoidal central living room at the center of the house. Moving around the chimney and into the angularly vaulted space, one became aware of the woodland beyond; the wings of the house seemed to embrace the expansive, tree-perforated deck just outside. The western wing of the house contained service, kitchen, and dining areas as well as a study, while the eastern wing contained bedrooms and baths. Through the geometry of her architecture, her choices of materials, and an open pattern of fenestration, Pettersen succeeded in making the house a part of the landscape—in almost any interior room one experienced a strong connection to the outdoors, which the house seemed to invite in.

Transition between entry court and front door, 1994. Photograph by R. Hruby. Courtesy JRC.

The large deck adjacent to the living room continued the indoor living space on grade outdoors. Projecting beyond the walls of the house, the deck was edged in part by timber benches, an original furniture design that Rose was frequently using in his gardens by this time. Their simple but clear tectonics and elegant scale belied the common and rough materials they were made of, exemplifying Rose's desire to create "something extraordinary with the commonplace, rather than something common with the extraordinary."[3]

A second deck led to a series of interlocking steps made of landscape timber risers and broken bluestone treads that con-

View from front of house toward entry court, 1994. Photograph by R. Hruby. Courtesy JRC.

nected the house to the forest floor roughly six feet beneath it, as well as to the house's lower level.[4] Rose designed these broad, wide steps to allow existing trees to remain within and around them as the steps gradually moved through the forest, inviting one to descend gracefully to the forest floor. This last, largest, and most complex part of the garden contained both a pool and a tennis court, along with pebble paths that sometimes doubled as drainage channels as they led one through the garden, as well as around the sides of the house and back to (or from) the parking court.

The pool and its attendant decking were irregular in form, with a sculptural Japanese black pine at the nexus

View from living room to decking at rear of house, 1994. Photograph by R. Hruby. Courtesy JRC.

Timber benches edging upper deck, 1994. Photograph by R. Hruby. Courtesy JRC.

of water and land. The similarities between this pool and
the one he had designed for the Averetts in Georgia almost
twenty-five years earlier were unmistakable. As pointed out
by Millicent Anisfield, her pool (like the Averetts') was not
designed for swimmers, as its geometry, while consistent
with the rest of the garden, precluded the swimming of traditional "laps."

Although Rose's characteristic angular geometry was
evident throughout the site, especially in his work with
hard-edged materials like timbers or dimension lumber, the
rounded native stones he scavenged from the site loosened
his space-forms. Also noteworthy is Rose's use of white peb-

Timber steps leading back toward decks and house, 2014. Photograph by Shanshan Yu. Courtesy JRC.

bles, sometimes embedded between the bluestone slabs, and round stones mined from the site to define walks that often also functioned as drainage channels. According to Jose Ferreira, Rose's foreman on later projects, Rose went out of his way to secure the white pebbles, importing them from Long Island for the Anisfields' and other gardens. Their color made them an unusual choice, suggesting that Rose, who was so inspired by his trips to Japan, may have been remembering the ancient Shinto practice of blessing the sites of shrines by spreading white pebbles on the ground around them; there certainly can be no doubt that the making of each garden was for Rose a spiritual experience.

According to Millicent Anisfield, "working with Jim was an experience in itself and added to the flavor of the house," though Rose did not talk to clients much anymore, preferring only to commune with the sites and to give specific instructions to the workers. Mrs. Anisfield recalls a moment when she had the temerity to ask Rose what he was going to do next in a particular area:

"I don't know" he replied and walked away. He didn't want you interfering. One day, as the project was finishing up, I walked in the driveway to the front and I noticed the way it was planted you couldn't

Pool with Japanese black pine, 1990. Photograph by George Peirce. © georgepeirce.com

Side path to rear decks and house, 1990. Photograph by George Peirce. © georgepeirce.com

see the front door. You wouldn't know where to go. And I said, "Jim, our friends will never find the front door." And this was not a man you criticized, not him or his work or anything else. And he looked at me, and for some reason we got along very well, and almost tongue in cheek he said to me, "So get new friends!"[5]

Today the garden is still maintained partly by Millicent Anisfield and one of the original crew who built it and remains very much as it was when Rose finished working on it in 1983, with one exception. According to Mrs. Anisfield,

sometime after 1983 deer began eating the hundreds of rhododendrons Rose had planted. Richard Anisfield spent years
replacing and adding to them before giving up and replanting the understory with hollies. While also broad-leaved and
evergreen, hollies are not the same as rhododendrons, however, and the indigenous character of the spaces suffers some
for it. Still, this garden is in very good condition as of this
writing, although its prospects for the future are unclear.

GLICKMAN GARDEN

ALLENDALE, NEW JERSEY

(1987)

By 1987, Rose, encouraged by his personal experiences with Japanese culture, had refined an approach initiated almost fifty years earlier, one characterized by an inherent frugality that dovetailed with a growing awareness of ecology in America, even as suburbia itself had spread. His long-held conviction to preserve and help to express the biophysical, "heavenly" character of sites by creating designed spatial experiences within them only became more entrenched with the continuing loss of natural resources all around him. In contrast, Rose wasted nothing: not the natural resources present on his sites, nor anything he could scavenge or repurpose from those sites or from the rest of suburbia; and certainly not any existing space on his clients' properties, nearly every inch of which he used to guide people's movement through what he hoped would be an inspiring spatial experience that would heighten perceptions of the integral character of nature and the self. Such creative conservation was distilled on smaller

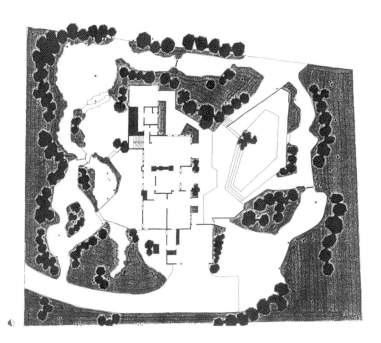

Figure-ground diagram, 1994.
Drawn by R. Hruby. Courtesy JRC.

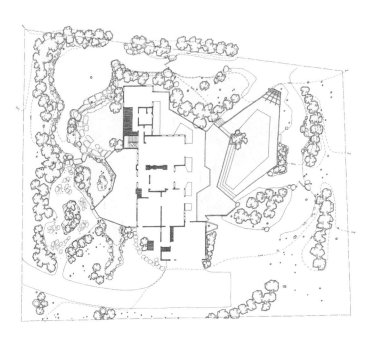

Plan, 1994. Drawn by
R. Hruby. Courtesy JRC.

properties, where precious natural resources and space, especially in the front of a house, were typically squandered in mindless lawns and decorative foundation plantings, because of archaic regulations and conventional thinking.

The Glickman site in Allendale, New Jersey, was one

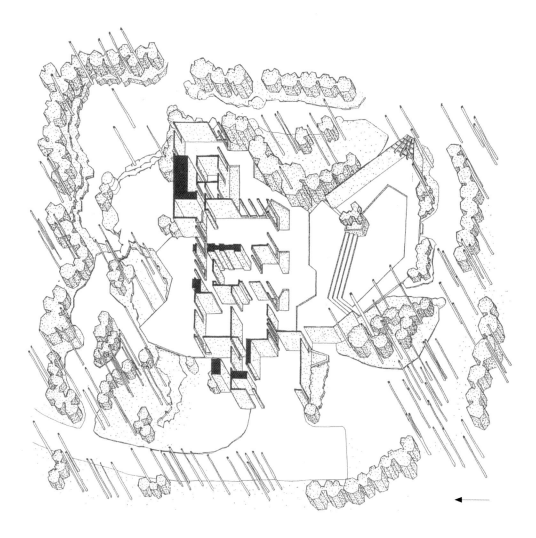

Axonometric plan, 1994. Drawn by R. Hruby. Courtesy JRC.

example of such a property. The three-quarter-acre site in an established, single-family residential neighborhood was relatively flat and wooded when Rose began work in 1986. As was the case with dozens of his later gardens, Rose was brought into the Glickman project by the architect Eleanore Pettersen. In her design of the unassuming two-thousand-square-foot house, Pettersen characteristically sought to disturb the site as little as possible while creating the opportunity for connecting double-height interior living spaces to a garden in the woods at the rear of the property through floor-to-ceiling, wall-to-wall glass. Owing to the site's relatively small size and the town's setback regulations, the house had to be located near the center of the lot, arbitrarily dividing the landscape. Siting the house in this way would typically result in the loss of the front of the property for any practical or spatial purpose, the forest replaced by a useless lawn sprawling from one property line to the other. As Rose described the deadening scene while panning a camera across the fronts of neighboring houses, "This is suburbia. If you haven't seen it, look left or right."[1]

There was no lawn or foundation planting at the front of the Glickman residence. (Indeed, one is hard-pressed to find a lawn in any of Rose's work.) Instead, Rose captured and used that space as part of the garden experience, a significant accomplishment at a site with only fifty feet between the house and the front (northern) property line. Along the street, as well as along the side and rear property lines, Rose closely planted masses of shade-tolerant native rhododendrons and hemlocks in the understory of the preserved forest. This established privacy and began to define space more clearly between the house, the street, and neighboring lots. Rose reconfigured this space into a kind of stroll garden leading to the front door, as well as to other spaces around

Entry from parking area to front yard, 1994. Photograph by R. Hruby. Courtesy JRC.

the house, including a series of decks around a pool at the rear of the property. Along the property's western side a driveway provided automobile access to an attached garage.

In the front one moved under the forest canopy, choreographed between and around the trunks of trees by additional native plantings (mostly rhododendrons) on segmented paths composed of large broken pieces of Pennsylvania bluestone, Long Island pebbles, and other stones Rose found on the site. Braided with the path was a (usually) dry streambed that also incorporated found rocks from the site in managing—and giving expression to—the movement of rainwater through the area. A large, obtuse-angled deck, formed around a cluster

Path to front door, 1994. Photograph by R. Hruby. Courtesy JRC.

of existing trees, bridged the streambed and linked the walk to the front door in two places. A bluestone bridge between branches of the path and a bluestone-edged pebble terrace just below the deck served similar purposes. These features wove through the forest, resolving in a small gathering space near the eastern property line. The now-fused pebble path / dry streambed then passed through one of two "rock ikebana" gateways as it led to the rear of the property.

Rose's guided walk in the woods continued around the eastern and southern sides of the house, culminating in the main gathering space in the back. It was into this space, over long, obtuse-angled decks, that Pettersen's interior living

Path and drainage way in front yard, 1994. Photograph by R. Hruby. Courtesy JRC.

View from front deck, 1994. Photograph by R. Hruby. Courtesy JRC.

Pool and decking looking northwest toward rear of house, 1991. Photograph by George Peirce. © georgepeirce.com.

Pool and decking looking southeast, 1994. Photograph by R. Hruby. Courtesy JRC.

and dining rooms overflowed. The space contained a long, angular swimming pool that was asymmetrically oriented to direct views away from the eastern neighbor's house and backyard. A reed-surfaced screen enclosed the pool on its eastern edge for additional privacy. The space culminated in a trellised sitting area, counterpoising an outdoor dining area on the opposite side of the terraced decks and pool. Between the upper deck and the pool were long, shallow steps, allowing direct entry into the water as well as access to an asymmetrical walk around the pool. A Japanese black pine and a saucer magnolia, arranged tightly together in a small, single planter, divided the steps and marked the break in form at the intersection of the stairs with the water. Masses of native rhododendrons to its south completed the definition of this outdoor living–dining room and continued to define the path through the woods. A second "rock ikebana" gateway led to the garage on the western side of the house, marking another route to the strolling garden, while a beautifully crafted screen and gate allowed for more direct access between the garage and the garden.

Throughout every inch of the strolling garden, including what would typically be the front lawn, Rose used his flexible, angular space-forms to define volumes and choreograph movement within the existing woods. As was evidenced here and at the Anisfield garden in Saddle River, New Jersey, Rose's angular forms softened and became looser when he defined space with native plants and stones, compared to when he was working with dimension lumber or landscape timbers. His use of the dry streambed to manage runoff was typical of his 1970s and 1980s gardens and was perhaps inspired by his respect for natural resources, as well as by some of the Japanese gardens he had visited, where symbolic water features actually did manage runoff when it rained.[2] The dry streambed

Gravel space/drainage device near eastern property line, 1994. Photograph by R. Hruby. Courtesy JRC.

at the Glickman residence, as in other of Rose's gardens of this period, served the ecological purpose of managing storm water on the site while remaining true to Rose's characteristically un-Japanese angular form and modern spatial sensibility; the streambed was woven into the choreographed spatial experience of the user as one moved over, around, and through it.

Since 1994 the Glickman garden has been owned by Gordon Borteck and Cheryl Rubin. Experienced today, it has lost some of its privacy and spatial clarity owing to the growth or death of some rhododendrons and trees. Despite the excellent maintenance provided by Borteck and Rubin, some of the front and rear decking is beginning to decay, and

Woven path and streambed, 1994. Photograph by R. Hruby. Courtesy JRC.

the reed screening along the pool terrace's eastern edge has been replaced more than once. A second (detached) garage–studio, designed by Eleanore Pettersen, was added at the end of the driveway in 1999. None of these changes, however, has had a significant impact on Rose's design intent, which, of course, acknowledged change as an inherent part of the life of a garden.

View from central shelter to eastern courtyard, James Rose Center, 2014. Photograph by author. Courtesy JRC.

THE JAMES ROSE
CENTER FOR LANDSCAPE
ARCHITECTURAL RESEARCH
AND DESIGN

(1991–PRESENT)

In his letter to the ASLA Classic Award jury, the landscape architect Richard Haag described the changing essence of Rose's design for his Ridgewood home.

> Many theoreticians would nominate Mies van der Rohe's Barcelona Pavilion as the most seminal building in Western architecture in this century, a true monument. In contrast the James Rose Center is a living organism never reaching perfection.
>
> Rose's enduring creation defies our incessant need to name everything, to put every object into a bit. But rather like nature, there is a continuous growth/decay, a middle state of being, encompassing but empty. Perhaps analogous to a Zen koan did James Rose pose such an obvious paradox, that the stress of meditation on its lasting contribution to the wellness of humankind is in itself illuminating.[1]

By 1991, Rose's family home had decayed considerably. On his death in late summer that year, a few of his friends began the work of converting the property into a landscape research and study center, something Rose had been looking into doing himself for some time. During 1992 and into 1993, the home remained unoccupied and in disrepair while an educational foundation was established and a plan developed. In summer 1993, Brian Higley and Meg Rasmussen, who had participated in the planning, were retained as part-time caretakers. They moved into Rose's deserted home, and over the next five years, under my direction and with the assistance of numerous volunteers, they began to rehuman-

Volunteers rebuilding woven fences at northern shelter, late 1990s. Photograph by author. Courtesy JRC.

Rebuilt bench, 1995. Photograph by author. Courtesy JRC.

ize the place, looking after it, making repairs, and helping to develop and implement programs for its educational use. As a carpenter and recent graduate of a landscape architecture program, Higley was able to make repairs in a sensitive way until the foundation could determine how to address the significant structural and mechanical failures.

It seemed like almost everything was broken or in decay when Higley and Rasmussen moved in. Among the first things Higley rebuilt was a low, elegant metal-and-wood bench visible from the main interior gathering space across the largest pool. During its reconstruction, Higley discovered that, true to form for Rose, this refined bench was actually made from an old door. All the leaking pools were rebuilt, with the old hose nozzles again making fountains when reattached to new submersible pumps. Student volunteers rebuilt and replanted the garden, reestablishing privacy on the eastern side of the property by adding more native

View looking south from Ridgewood Avenue, 2000. Photograph by author. Courtesy JRC.

rhododendrons, hemlocks, and Japanese black pines to the surviving ones.

On the western side, adjacent to Southern Parkway, the woven cedar fence had rotted and collapsed; it was rebuilt using as much of the original wood as could be salvaged, along with new cedar planks and posts, and eventually all of the perimeter fences were reconstructed. Rose's *River of Hospitality* mural, covering a portion of an outside wall and continuing through a door onto an inside wall, was restored.[2] A furnace was replaced, leaks were stopped, and the main shelter became habitable again, while numerous other smaller but significant

Reconstructed *River of Hospitality* mural, 2000. Photograph by author. Courtesy JRC.

measures were taken so that Rose's space-sculpture-with-shelter could be opened to the public for tours. The Center began a modest research and educational program, including a student internship program, a documentation project, and the establishment of an archive and a lecture series.

In 1993, Matthew Barry, a landscape architecture student, followed in 1995 by Monica Balabani, also a student, produced new measured plans of the site, documenting the many changes Rose had made to his original 1952–1953 design. In the summer of 1995, Deborah Wallstrom, an intern at the Center, using scraps of old family photos and the precious few other historical documents Rose had kept, pieced together a technical record of the changes that had occurred since Ridgewood's original construction. During the first few summers after Rose's death, numerous volunteers and student interns repaired and rebuilt his improvisations and renovations, even as many other parts of the Ridgewood home continued to decay. Bob Hruby, Anna-Maria Vissilia, Karen Krolewski, Peter Witke, and other students documented several of Rose's unknown projects from the later part of his career as part of the Center's ongoing James Rose Garden Documentation Project.

In 1998–1999, following passage of the New Jersey Rehabilitation Subcode, the Center initiated major repairs

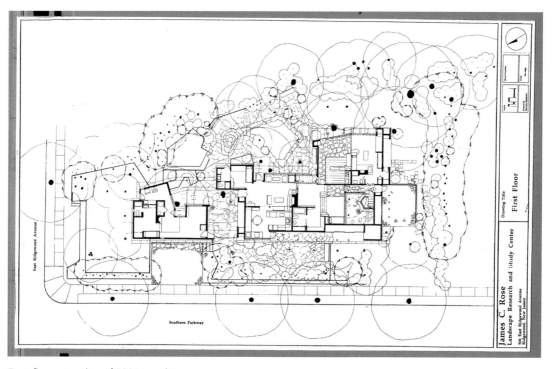

First-floor site plan of 2001 condition. Drawn by M. Balabani, 2005, after M. Barry. Courtesy JRC.

to the Ridgewood property.[3] Brian Higley and Meg Rasmussen had moved on by this time, and the landscape architecture graduate Krista Murphy and her husband, Mark Woitkiewicz, were assisting with the caretaking and management of the Center during renovations. Much of the roof garden was removed so that leaking roofs could be replaced and other structural deficiencies remedied. Parts of the roof garden were then rebuilt almost exactly as they had been, with many of the existing materials used in the reconstruction. The north studio, originally Rose's part of the family enclave, was fully restored with a new kitchen and other improvements consistent with Rose's design, so that it could once again be rented or occupied by a care-

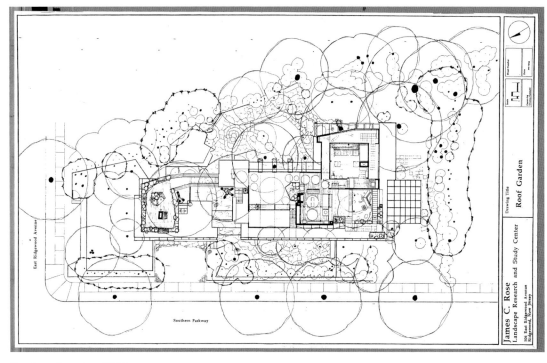

Roof garden plan, 2005. Drawn by M. Balabani. Courtesy JRC.

Volunteers replanting rebuilt roof garden over northern shelter, 2000. Photograph by author. Courtesy JRC.

taker. These renovations were performed by Ken Kral, a building contractor who, along with his father, had worked as a carpenter on some of Rose's other projects in the area.

As its program expanded in subsequent years to include competitions and exhibitions, the Center continued renovations, including numerous repairs to the masonry and woodwork by reconstruction specialist Rob Thompson, and tradesmen Bruce Mason and Ken Buxton. In 2003, using Rose's 1952 plan and the 1992 Barry plan, as well as evidence still present on-site, students Yen-I Han and Josh Coroa constructed physical models of the property's design to compare its condition in 1953 and 2003. These models remain useful tools at the Center, serving as bookends to the property's metamorphosis and helping provoke visitors to visualize its dynamic history.

In 2007 the town of Ridgewood shut down the James Rose Center for operating an educational program in a residential zone, threatening its continued existence. The foundation immediately sought a variance. At the hearing, many of Ridgewood's citizens spoke on the Center's behalf. Significantly, those who testified included young architects and landscape architects who attributed their interest in their new careers to internships they had held at the Center or visits they had made there while growing up in the community. The variance was granted in 2008.

Since then the foundation has struggled to maintain the property while continuing its research and educational

Visitors at *Suburbia Transformed* exhibition, 2014. Photograph by author. Courtesy JRC.

Zendo, 1996. Photograph by Frederick Charles. © fcharles.com

program and reopening Rose's personal refuge seasonally to the general public. A visit today exposes decades
of "continuous growth/decay," embodying the story of
Rose's evolving life and times. It can be read "between the
lines drawn by materials," in an opalescent light stream-
ing through the lindens and the fiberglass screens. There,
behind the layers of glass and block, the broad-leaved evergreens, unraveling woven fences, and an indomitable "pole
arrangement," the din of suburbia subsides and the hiss of
scrap metal serpents fills the air.

NOTES

OVERVIEW

1. Katherine Whiteside, "Zensational," *Elle Décor,* October/November 1995, 218.
2. James C. Rose, *Creative Gardens* (New York: Reinhold, 1958), 21.
3. The story of the "Harvard Revolt" led by Rose, Garrett Eckbo, and Daniel Urban Kiley is told in several publications, but perhaps nowhere as dramatically as in Rose's own *Modern American Gardens— Designed by James Rose* (New York: Reinhold, 1967), 17–25.
4. For *Pencil Points,* Rose wrote "Freedom in the Garden," 19 (October 1938): 640–44. "Plants Dictate Garden Forms," 19 (November 1938): 695–97; "Integration," 19 (December 1938): 758–60; "Articulate Form in Landscape Design," 20 (February 1939): 98–100; "Plant Forms and Space," 20 (April 1939): 226–30; "Landscape Models," 20 (July 1939): 438–48; and "Why Not Try Science," 20 (December 1939): 777–79. For *California Arts and Architecture:* "Gardens," 57 (May 1940), 20; "1+1=5," 57 (June/July 1940): 38, 46; "The Hanging Garden," 57 (August 1940): 25; "This Garden Is the Garden for You," 57 (October 1940): 26; "Bogeys in the Landscape," 57 (November 1940): 27, 38; "Outdoor Theater," 58 (January 1941): 29; "When a House Is Not a Home," 58 (March 1941): 27; "Are You a Plant Snob," 58 (April 1941): 30, 46; and "Garden Details," 58 (July 1941): 28–29, 38–39. For *Architectural Record,* written with Daniel Kiley and Garrett Eckbo: "Landscape Design in the Urban Environment," 85 (May 1939):

70–77; "Landscape Design in the Rural Environment," 86 (August 1939): 68–74; and "Landscape Design in the Primeval Environment," 87 (February 1940): 74–79.

5. Rose, in discussion with the author, July 1991.

6. These are phrases Rose used to describe his built projects and to organize the chapters in his first book, *Creative Gardens*.

7. Rose, in discussion with the author, July 1991.

8. Rose was indirectly exposed to Japanese design culture long before 1960, in large measure through his close association with Christopher Tunnard and Antonin Raymond. It has been implied that he was first exposed to Japan while stationed at Okinawa during World War II, but Rose angrily refuted this, insisting that his first real exposure was through WoDeCo.

9. James C. Rose, *Gardens Make Me Laugh* (Norwalk, CT: Silvermine, 1965), 21.

10. Elizabeth K. Meyer to ASLA Classic Award jury, May 11, 1999, and Peter Walker to ASLA Classic Award jury, May 11, 1999, James Rose Center Archives (JRCA).

11. Rose, "Bogeys in the Landscape," 27.

12. Rose, undated notebook, JRCA.

13. Late in his life Rose often quoted Thoreau on civil disobedience, self-reliance, nature, and spirituality, all of which clearly resonated with his own life and work. While during the first phase of his career Rose championed the "modern" character of landscape architecture, he did not renounce its connection to an American transcendentalist view of nature. This perspective found increasing voice in his later life and work in tandem with his discovery of Zen Buddhism, as well as his anger at the American attitudes, institutions, policies, and regulations he saw as responsible for the destruction of the natural environment that accompanied postwar suburbanization.

14. Rose's father, Clarence, worked in construction, and during Rose's youth he often left the family for extended periods to find work in upstate New York.

15. Marc Snow [James Rose], *Modern American Gardens—Designed by James Rose* (New York: Reinhold, 1967), 14–15.

16. Rose, "Freedom in the Garden," 641.

17. Kim Levin, "Farewell to Modernism," *Arts Magazine* 54 (October 1979): 90–91.

18. William Carlos Williams, XXII, *Spring and All* (Paris: Contact, 1923).

19. Rose's theatrical nature, as well as his passion for playwriting, acting, and attending the theater, permeated his early life. He vigorously encouraged his mother to go into the theater, often reading with her, and seriously considered doing so himself. The theatrical atmosphere at the Rose compound would later inspire his colleague Eleanore Pet-

tersen to characterize the scene there as being like "something out of Tennessee Williams." Rose wrote several unpublished plays and became deeply interested in Noh theater after going to Japan. Late in his life, I witnessed Rose preparing to go to his worksites as if he were about to go onstage. He saw himself as both actor and playwright in the spontaneously unfolding adventure that was, to him, the landscape drama.

20. James Rose (JR) to Minnie Rose (MR), March 12, 1933, JRCA.
21. Snow, *Modern American Gardens,* 78.
22. Kathryn Smith, *Schindler House* (Santa Monica, CA: Hennessey & Ingalls, 2010), 7.
23. Snow, *Modern American Gardens,* 15.
24. Maurice Besset, *Le Corbusier,* trans. Robin Kemball (New York: Skira/Rizzoli, 1987), 65.
25. Snow, *Modern American Gardens,* 81.
26. The Bauhaus was a design school that Gropius founded in Weimar, Germany, in 1919 as a place for the integration of all the modern arts and crafts, including architecture. Significantly, landscape architecture was not included, nor was it addressed in the school's curricula.
27. Catherine Howett, "Modernism and American Landscape Architecture," in *Modern Landscape Architecture: A Critical Review,* ed. Marc Treib (Cambridge, MA: MIT Press, 1993), 30.
28. Snow, *Modern American Gardens,* 13, 15, 16.
29. Fletcher Steele, "Landscape Design of the Future," *Landscape Architecture* 22 (July 1932): 299–300.
30. Snow, *Modern American Gardens,* 78, 81.
31. Dan Kiley, in discussion with the author, March 1992.
32. Rose, "Gardens," 20.
33. Garrett Eckbo to the author, August 1, 1994, JRCA.
34. Snow, *Modern American Gardens,* 17, 19.
35. For a discussion of the beginnings of Harvard's Graduate School of Design, see Jill Pearlman, *Inventing American Modernism* (Charlottesville: University of Virginia Press, 2007).
36. Christopher Tunnard had been writing articles about modern landscapes in England before he was imported to the GSD. He combined these articles into a significant book, *Gardens in the Modern Landscape,* in 1938. While at Harvard, Tunnard and Rose became particularly close, spending many weekends together in New York and, after Harvard, traveling together across the country to California.
37. Rose, in discussion with the author, July 1991.
38. Ibid.
39. Rose, "Freedom in the Garden," 640.
40. Since Rose, Kiley, and Eckbo enthusiastically engaged the subject of space in the landscape, its essence has been explored and its nature

illuminated by scholars and theoreticians, including Ernö Goldfinger, Philip Thiel, Patrick Condon, and Joseph S. R. Volpe. For a particularly interesting definition of modern landscape space, see Condon's "Cubist Space, Volumetric Space, and Landscape Architecture," *Landscape Journal* 7, no. 1 (1988): 1–14, as well as the subsequent discussion between Condon and Lawrence Halprin on the subject, found in *Landscape Journal* 8, no. 2 (1989): 151–52.

41. Rose, "Articulate Form in Landscape Design," 100.
42. Rose, "Freedom in the Garden," 642.
43. Rose, "Plants Dictate Garden Forms," 695, 697.
44. Rose, "Articulate Form in Landscape Design," 98.
45. Rose, "Landscape Models," 438.
46. Snow, *Modern American Gardens*, 87.
47. Rose, "Landscape Models," 438.
48. A. E. Bye, "Dangerous Ground for the Uninformed," *Landscape Architecture* 58 (October 1968): 51.
49. Snow, *Modern American Gardens*, 83.
50. Rose, "Integration," 759.
51. Snow, *Modern American Gardens*, 20, 23.
52. Rose, "Freedom in the Garden," 642.
53. Rose, *Creative Gardens*, 22.
54. JR to MR, March 23, 1940, JRCA.
55. In 1941, the Dickinson garden, which appears to have been Rose's first professional commission, was executed in Pasadena for $1,200.
56. Raymond had worked for Frank Lloyd Wright on the Imperial Hotel in Tokyo, in which city Raymond also established a practice and became known as the father of modern architecture. Raymond's appreciation for Japanese culture and design permeated his life and work, and Rose no doubt had a powerful if indirect introduction to Japan through Raymond. After World War II, Rose continued to collaborate with Raymond and to benefit from associations with the people he met in New Hope, including Junzo Yoshimura and George Nakashima. In *Creative Gardens*—in a moment of uncharacteristic humility—Rose refers to Raymond as his "master" (134).
57. Snow, *Modern American Gardens*, 95.
58. Ibid.
59. JR to MR, May 12, 1943, JRCA.
60. JR to MR, December 18, 1944, JRCA.
61. JR to MR, November 5, 1944, JRCA.
62. JR to MR, December 9, 1944, JRCA.
63. James Rose, *The Heavenly Environment—A Landscape Drama in Three Acts with a Backstage Interlude* (Hong Kong: New City Cultural Service, 1987), 122.
64. JR to MR, April 26, 1945, JRCA.

65. JR to MR, August 11, 1945, JRCA.

66. Eleanore Pettersen, in discussion with the author, June 1992.

67. Many of the projects, drawings, and photographs that Rose used in composing *Creative Gardens* were first published in the magazines and periodicals for which he wrote both before and immediately after the war. Projects completed between 1946 and 1958 include Rose's "modular gardens" (1947), on which he was assisted by his young employee Cornelia Hahn (later Cornelia Hahn Oberlander); the Krakauer and Rosen garden (1946–1947) in collaboration with Antonin Raymond; the Lapkin garden (1951) in Montvale, New Jersey, which was the first of many projects integrated with houses designed concurrently by Frank Lloyd Wright's apprentice Eleanore Pettersen; and the Wurtzburger Sculpture Garden at Timberlane in Pikesville, Maryland (1956), an outdoor "space-sculpture" containing object sculptures by Henry Moore, Auguste Rodin, and Jacques Lipchitz among others. During this period Rose also completed two house-and-garden designs ("space-sculptures-with-shelters," as he called them): the Macht residence (1956) in Baltimore, and his own family home (1952–1953) in Ridgewood, New Jersey. By 1958 he had also executed garden commissions in South Orange, West Orange, Livingston, Metuchen, Hillsdale, and Morristown, New Jersey; New Rochelle, Kings Point, Ossining, and Roslyn, New York; Norwich, Connecticut; and Miami, Florida, among other cities.

68. For Rose's explication of his encounters with his first and subsequent book publishers, see *Heavenly Environment,* 164–68.

69. Rose's commitment to designing with three-dimensional physical models has already been elaborated on; however, unlike in his pre-war articles, in his first book Rose declined to use photographs of the models he had made for his projects. Since by that time he had photographs of the projects as built, he may have decided that photographs of models were no longer useful to the story he was trying to compose. The photographers for *Creative Gardens* included some of the era's best architectural photographers, such as Ezra Stoller. Rose produced most of the sketches for the book, whereas many of the axonometric plans were by Charles Rieger, an architect Rose had met while lecturing at Columbia.

70. Rose, *Creative Gardens,* 22.

71. Ibid.

72. "Blacktop," as Rose and others referred to it, was a durable asphalt road surface introduced in the United States in the 1920s. Inexpensive and, when properly blended, permeable, Rose found it to be a serviceable and affordable, if startling, material to use in his gardens.

73. For a more detailed description of the Krakauer and Rosen resi-

dences, which included Rose's earliest known use of railroad ties, see Caroline Rob Zaleski, *Long Island Modernism, 1930–1980* (New York: Norton, 2012), 62.

74. *Fountain* was a urinal that Duchamp inscribed "R. Mutt 1917" and intended to display on a pedestal as part of a show in New York sponsored by the Society of Independent Artists (of which Duchamp was a member). Another example of a work in which a common object is redefined by being placed in a new context is Kurt Schwitters's *Rubbish Construction,* cited by Rose in "Freedom in the Garden."

75. Garrett Eckbo to the author, August 1, 1994, JRCA.

76. See Rose, "Freedom in the Garden," 642.

77. Rose, *Creative Gardens,* 50.

78. Ibid., 51.

79. Rose, "Plant Forms and Space," 227.

80. Rose, *Creative Gardens,* 171.

81. Rose, *Gardens Make Me Laugh,* 66.

82. Ibid., 67.

83. Ibid., 85, 74.

84. Ibid., 81.

85. Michael Van Valkenburgh, *Built Landscapes: Gardens in the Northeast* (Brattleboro, VT: Brattleboro Museum and Art Center, 1984), 43.

86. Snow, *Modern American Gardens,* 5.

87. Rose, in discussion with the author, July 1991.

88. Rose, *Heavenly Environment,* 164–65.

89. Ibid., 165.

90. Rose, unpublished notes for *Heavenly Environment,* JRCA.

91. Rose, *Heavenly Environment,* 86–88.

92. James Rose, *The Heavenly Environment and Other Crimes: Thoughts and Comments of James Rose, Landscape Architect* (1986; Ridgewood, NJ: James Rose Center, 2005), DVD video.

93. About a quarter of these projects have been documented since his death, and few remain in good condition. Rose's withdrawal from society, his general contempt for historiography and biography, and his unorthodox "paperless" design methods have resulted in a far from complete record of his work being available. The James Rose Center has rediscovered several of his built works since his death. Doubtless there are more to be found.

94. Eleanore Pettersen, in discussion with the author, June 1992.

95. Ibid.

96. Jose Ferreira, in discussion with the author, July 1991.

97. Rose, *The Heavenly Environment and Other Crimes.*

98. Rose, *Heavenly Environment,* 123.

99. Ibid., 156.

100. Rose, *The Heavenly Environment and Other Crimes.*

101. Rose, in discussion with the author and others at the Tremaine garden, June 1990.
102. Rose, "Plant Forms and Space," 227–28.
103. Rose's letters to his mother during the war indicate that his eyes were examined for color deficiency, although medical authorities concluded he was not color blind.
104. Rose, in discussion with the author at the Van Ness garden, June 1990.
105. Rose, *Heavenly Environment,* 106.
106. These friends included Leon Shipper, William Zagorski, Jose Ferreira, and Dean Cardasis; Lawrence Rappaport and Frank Carrabba also gave their assistance.

DICKINSON GARDEN AND HOUSE

1. James C. Rose, "Gardens," *California Arts and Architecture* 57 (May 1940): 20.
2. Lawrence Test (1891–1981), a junior draftsman with Reginald Johnson before graduating from the University of Pennsylvania's school of architecture, would become a modern designer later in his career. Woodbridge Dickinson graduated with a degree in architecture from Harvard's Graduate School of Design in 1938 and may have known Rose from their shared experience at Harvard.
3. In 1946 Rose was commissioned by the *Ladies' Home Journal* to do a series of small gardens. He proposed a modular system of standardized garden units, including exposed aggregate concrete pavers, much like those used at the Dickinson residence, along with walls and space dividers, trellis members, pools, and plant forms in a system that could be produced and assembled in various combinations for the magazine, as well as mass produced for the average postwar home grounds. His ideas for modular landscape designs were published in two theoretical articles in *Progressive Architecture* in 1947. Rose also republished these examples in *Creative Gardens* in 1958, suggesting that—more than a decade after first conceiving of modular landscape design—he still believed in the idea of a generally applicable landscape system that the public could employ. By the early 1960s, however, Rose had renounced the idea, since it precluded the evolution of an organic form which could and should evolve from, as well as express, the specific and particular conditions of the site.
4. James C. Rose, *Creative Gardens* (New York: Reinhold, 1958), 67.
5. Ibid., 66.
6. Ibid., 68.
7. "House in California," *Architectural Forum* 85 (November 1946): 90.
8. Rose had traveled to California from the East Coast with his close friend Christopher Tunnard, a landscape architect and garden designer

whose project with architect Serge Chermayeff at Bentley Wood in Halland, East Sussex, England, was first published in the United States in Tunnard's book *Gardens in the Modern Landscape* in 1938.

ROSE GARDEN AND HOUSE (PART 1)

1. At the time that Rose built his home, Ridgewood was a well-established suburb (17,500 people in 1950) in the foothills of the Ramapo and Watchung Mountains, with few remaining buildable tracts of land. Twenty-five years earlier, Rose's site had been an old North Jersey Transit Company trolley stop along a line that ran adjacent to the Ho-Ho-Kus Brook, linking Paterson to Mahwah. In 1952 the site was overgrown; east of the trolley line had become a utility right-of-way, while Ridgewood Avenue and Southern Parkway bordered the site on its north and west sides, respectively. Rose's site was less than a quarter of an acre, a trapezoid of long, narrow proportions that was not considered to be particularly suitable for building.
2. "Open House for the Benefit of Village School for Retarded Children," James Rose Center Archives. Interestingly, at the end of this brochure Rose, who had cunningly circumscribed what he considered to be the town's intrusive regulations, trumpets that there "has been no violation of Ridgewood's Building Code."
3. James C. Rose, "My Connecticut Home and Garden Began in Okinawa," *American Home* 36 (October 1946): 20.
4. Ibid., 22.
5. Ibid.
6. James C. Rose, *Creative Gardens* (New York: Reinhold, 1958), 111.
7. James C. Rose, "Plant Forms and Space," *Pencil Points* 20 (April 1939): 227.
8. The editors of *Progressive Architecture* already had experience with Rose's writings, since *Pencil Points* had merged with *Progressive Architecture* in 1943. *Progressive Architecture* frequently featured Rose and his work and remained the voice of modern and avant-garde architecture and design until 1996, when it was bought by a competitor and discontinued.
9. "A Traditional Japanese House: The Esthetic Discipline," *Progressive Architecture* 35 (December 1954): 109; "A Contemporary American House: The Spatial Discipline," *Progressive Architecture* 35 (December 1954): 114.
10. James Rose, *The Heavenly Environment—A Landscape Drama in Three Acts with a Backstage Interlude* (Hong Kong: New City Cultural Service, 1987), 96.
11. Rose, *Creative Gardens,* 111.
12. Such as "Falling Leaves," described later in this essay.

13. In Ludwig Mies van der Rohe's 1929 Barcelona Pavilion, the architect famously extended the solid walls of his building to begin to define space outdoors. Rose did something similar at Ridgewood, but unlike Mies, who made the walls of his elegant minimalist structure out of marble, Rose used common concrete block to make the walls at his middle-class home.

14. Rose, *Creative Gardens,* 108.

15. Rose continued to use this furniture at his home throughout his life. However, the woven cord became too difficult to replace, and he eventually reclad the frames with mahogany. After Rose's death, the mahogany versions of these chairs and benches were rebuilt by Brian Higley during his tenure as caretaker of the property, on restored metal frames found at Rose's house. In 2014, the efforts of Michael Van Valkenburgh Associates, Landscape Forms, and the James Rose Center to adapt Rose's original bench design to contemporary fabrication won an ASLA award for adaptation of a historically significant artifact to contemporary materials and means of mass production. As of this writing Michael Van Valkenburgh is planning to use the bench in some of his projects.

16. James C. Rose, "Freedom in the Garden," *Pencil Points* 19 (October 1938): 642.

17. Marc Snow [James Rose], *Modern American Gardens—Designed by James Rose* (New York: Reinhold, 1967), 154.

MACHT GARDEN AND HOUSE

1. Information from Lois Macht, in discussion with the author, November 1, 2014; she was not able to provide additional details about the commission.

2. James C. Rose, *Creative Gardens* (New York: Reinhold, 1958), 135.

3. "Houses and Landscapes," *Progressive Architecture* (May 1960): 163.

4. Rose, *Creative Gardens,* 135.

5. Ibid., 136.

6. Ibid.

7. Lois Macht discussion with the author.

8. Ibid.

9. Ibid.

10. "A Total Environment That Fosters a New Pattern of Living," *House and Garden* (January 1961): 66.

AVERETT GARDEN AND HOUSE

1. Mary Keith Averett in discussion with the landscape historian James Cochran and the Yarbroughs on the occasion of a visit to her for-

mer home in fall 2005. Document contained in MSS 989, James R. Cothran Papers, James G. Kenan Research Center, Atlanta History Center, Atlanta, Georgia.

2. Sidney and Rebecca Yarbrough, in discussion with the author, August 26, 2014.

3. Averett–Cochran discussion.

4. Marc Snow [James Rose], *Modern American Gardens—Designed by James Rose* (New York: Reinhold, 1967), 132–33.

5. Such an integral pool form was already becoming a characteristic feature of many of Rose's projects and can be seen in many subsequent works, such as the 1983 Anisfield garden. As this interlocking form developed, Rose would more likely mark the intersection between water and land with a Japanese black pine or a sculptural fountain derived from the "snake dance" fountain he created for a German landscape exposition, as described in the G-V Controls essay.

6. Snow, *Modern American Gardens,* 133.

7. Averett–Cochran discussion.

8. Sidney and Rebecca Yarbrough, in discussion with the author, August 26, 2014.

G-V CONTROLS COURTYARD

1. G-V Controls was one of Rose's few corporate commissions, along with General Signals (1976) in Stamford, Connecticut, and Texwipe (1985) in Saddle River, New Jersey.

2. Marc Snow [James Rose], *Modern American Gardens—Designed by James Rose* (New York: Reinhold, 1967), 9.

3. Ibid., 11.

4. Ibid., 18.

5. Ibid., 22.

ROSE GARDEN AND HOUSE (PART 2)

1. According to the U.S. Bureau of Labor Consumer Price Index, $24,000 in 1967 was equivalent to about $172,000 in 2016.

2. It is the habit of white pines as they grow to shade out and therefore lose their own lower branches. This had happened during the sixteen years since Rose had planted the white pines, which meant that they no longer screened the increasingly busy roads north and west of the site. Rose did not remove the pines, however, but simply added the fences just outside their trunks.

3. With his studio often rented and Minnie no longer living, when Rose was in town he stayed in the main house, which was otherwise occupied by his sister Jean.

4. James Rose, in discussion with the author, August 1991.

5. Ibid.

6. In *Creative Gardens* (New York: Reinhold, 1958), Rose tells of how he circumvented the building code restriction against high fences and landscape screens by configuring utilities and storage as enclosed parts of the "house." Then he used these enclosed storage closets to define space for Minnie's bedroom garden, which the closet walls screened from the neighbors and Southern Parkway. It was against one such wall that he built the new stairway to the roof garden (111).

7. James C. Rose, *The Heavenly Environment—A Landscape Drama in Three Acts with a Backstage Interlude* (Hong Kong: New City Cultural Service, 1987), 112.

8. See the Paley, Anisfield, and Glickman essays for explication.

9. This was Mrs. Werlin, at whose residence in 1986 Rose converted a swampland into a water garden.

PALEY GARDEN

1. James C. Rose, *The Heavenly Environment—A Landscape Drama in Three Acts with a Backstage Interlude* (Hong Kong: New City Cultural Service, 1987), 56.

2. See ibid., 56 and 60–61, for Rose's story of how he and Florence Paley were able to save the existing forest from the ravages of the conventional construction process.

3. In *The Heavenly Environment* Rose titles his description of this garden "The Medea Touch," comparing his client to Medea, a sorceress in Greek mythology and the subject of several Greek tragedies, to illustrate how a character can influence an outcome and how "essence" is revealed in both Greek tragedy and landscape design.

4. Ibid., 61.

5. James Rose, *The Heavenly Environment and Other Crimes* (1986; Ridgewood, NJ: James Rose Center, 2005), DVD.

6. For the Documentation Project, see Anisfield essay, note 1.

ANISFIELD GARDEN

1. The Anisfeld garden was among the first of Rose's undocumented works recorded by Bob Hruby and Anna-Maria Vissilia under my supervision as part of the James Rose Garden Documentation Project. The resulting documentation packages—comprising drawings, photographs, and written descriptions of several James Rose gardens—are now part of the archives of the James Rose Center.

2. Mike Ruepp's father, Henry, was also a mason and also worked for Rose; after Henry died in 1981, Mike continued to do much of the

bluestone paving for Rose over the next decade. The Anisfield garden, along with the nearby and simultaneously built VanNess garden, were among Mike's first solo efforts.

3. James Rose, in discussion with the author, July 1991.

4. These steps as well as the benches Rose constructed in this garden were made from landscape timbers because real railroad ties had become more difficult to obtain. Such was the case in many of Rose's gardens of this period and throughout the remainder of his career.

5. Millicent Anisfield, in discussion with the author, July 31, 2014.

GLICKMAN GARDEN

1. James Rose, *The Heavenly Environment and Other Crimes* (1986; Ridgewood, NJ: James Rose Center, 2005), DVD.

2. Examples include the famous moss garden at Saihō-ji in Kyoto, where a symbolic waterfall becomes a real waterfall during a storm, and the lesser-known Manshu-in (also in Kyoto), where the symbolic dry stream swells into a pebbled "pool" that actually functions as a dry well.

THE JAMES ROSE CENTER FOR LANDSCAPE ARCHITECTURAL RESEARCH AND DESIGN

1. Richard Haag, letter to ASLA Classic Award jury, May 4, 1999, James Rose Center Archives.

2. In the mid-1950s, Rose planned a mosaic mural for the concrete block wall that extended through a floor-to-ceiling glass wall between the dining area and the kitchen courtyard to its east. See *Creative Gardens* (p. 115) for a description of the mural, which he titles *River of Hospitality*. The mural was constructed shortly thereafter and modified during the major renovations of 1968 to extend along the outside eastern wall of the kitchen area.

3. Adopted in 1998, the New Jersey Rehabilitation Subcode made it possible for properties listed on the state's register of historic places to be rehabilitated in keeping with their original design, rather than in accordance with new building codes. Thus the Center was able to preserve the character of Rose's home, which had been added to the register the year before.

INDEX

Page numbers in *italics* refer to illustrations.

Averett garden (*continued*)
trees, 137; oasis in, 140; pool
in, 135, *139,* 140, *142, 145,*
192; use of local pebbles in,
136; recycled materials in,
140; revised plan of, 133-35

Barardo, Rui (foreman), 77; firm
as Rose's Entourage, 182
Barcelona Pavilion (Mies van der
Rohe), 21, 24; as seminal
building, 209, 229n13
Barr, Alfred H., Jr., 33
Barry, Matthew, measured plans
by, 213, 216
Bauhaus (Weimer, Germany),
24, 40, 41; architects, 21, 39;
definition of, 223n26
Beaux-Arts: as style, 5, 8, 31; as
teaching method or system,
36-37, 161; tradition of, 27,
31-33
Bentley Wood (East Sussex,
England), 228n8; use of
screens to frame views, 98,
99
Black Mountain College (NC),
stop on East Coast road trip,
42
blacktop: definition of, 225n72;
permeable nature of, 82,
129, 130; special formula
of, 132; as surprising
material, 58, 60, 120. *See
also* asphalt
bluestone: as bridge, 202; in
later projects, 82; in paving,
171, 185, 201, 231-32n2; as
steps, 188, 190; in surface
compositions, 186, 193; in
terracing and pools, 171, 202
Borteck, Gordon, 206
Breuer, Marcel, 31

Buxton, Ken, 216
Bye, A. E., review of *Modern
American Gardens,* 38,
224n48

California Arts and Architecture:
articles in, 8, 29, 43, 91; on
Thomas Church, 27; on
cultural moment, 29
Cambridge (MA), 30, 31, 32
Camp Kilmer (NJ), military
staging area design for, 44
Carrabba, Frank, 227n106
Chermayeff, Serge, 98, 228n8
Church, Thomas: Rose
appreciation of, 27; and
Sullivan garden, *28;* 38; as
transitional figure, 27
Cochran, James, 229n1, 230n3, 7
Columbia University, 52
common materials, use of, 58-59,
120, 129, 132, 151, 190. *See
also* recycled materials
concrete: in blocks with steel,
117; in modular grid, 95;
as paving, 82, 94, *112,* 116,
129, 140, 186, 227n3; with
pebble aggregate, 135; as
walls in Rose house, *112,*
115-16, 228-29n13
Condon, Patrick, 224n40
conservation, in Rose's gardens,
11, 85, 197
Construction Spherique (Naum
Gabo), 33
Constructivists, 16, 19; work
admired by Rose, 41, 117
Cornell University, 5, 18, 30
Coroa, Josh, 216
Cooper Union: Eleanore
Pettersen as student at, 74;
Rose's teaching at, 52
Creative Gardens (1958), 8,

52, 118, 222n6, 225n67;
approach to building on-
site, 107; axonometric
plans, 100, 110, 123; client's
reading of, 133; concept
of landscape space, 56;
diagram of conventional
site development, *114;*
Dickinson garden, 93, 100;
fusion of architecture and
landscape, 116; garden as
sculpture, 41, 107; Macht
garden, 126, 130; Rose's
philosophy of gardens,
58, 61-63; mural, 232n2;
Antonin Raymond in,
224n56; republished articles,
227n3; Rose house site, 111,
113; story of circumventing
building codes, 231n6;
summary of, 54. *See also*
Freedman, Lionel; Stoller,
Ezra; Wasco, Lonnie
Cubism and Abstract Art (1936), 33
Cubists, description of, 16

Dadaists, description of, 16
Davenport, Butler, Free Theater,
Rose as member of, 42
Dedwylder, Rozier, 133, 144
Delaware River: Rose's home
site, 47; symbol of Rose's
heritage, 14, 18, 86
DeWitt Clinton High School, 15;
failure to graduate from, 30
Dickinson garden and house
(Pasadena, CA), 91-102,
224n55; concrete pavers in,
227n3; condition of, 101;
description of site in *Creative
Gardens,* 93; experiments
with space, 99; modular
paving, 93, 101; preservation

of existing features, 78; publication in *Architectural Forum* and *Creative Gardens,* 100; terraces and steps, 78

Dickinson, Mrs. Thompson, 92, 97; as collaborator in creating indoor–outdoor space, 101

Dickinson, Woodbridge, Jr., 93; as designer, 101; Harvard experience, 227n2

drainage devices: doubling as paths, *79,* 191, 193, *203;* gravel space in Glickman garden, *206*

Duchamp, Marcel, *Fountain,* 60, 226n74

ecology: aspect of James Rose Center programs, 86; definition *in Modern American Gardens,* 67; growing awareness of in America, 197

Eckbo, Garrett: coauthor of *Architectural Record* essays, 8, 221n4; friendship with Rose, 30, 32, 61; *Landscape for Living,* 52; Rose's visit with Tunnard, 42; trio with Rose and Kiley, 3, 25, 26, 30, 31, 221n3, 223n40

Einstein, Albert, 16

Exposition Internationale des Arts Decoratifs et Industriels Modernes (Paris, 1925), 24, *25,* 26

"Falling Leaves" (improvisation), 117, *119*

Faulkner, William, and modernism, 17

Ferreira, Jose (foreman), 77, 193, 226n96, 227n106

fiberglass, use of, 58, 120, 168-69, 219

found objects. *See* gardens: use of found objects in

Frank Grad and Sons, 147

Freedman, Lionel, photographs in *Creative Gardens,* 111

"Freedom in the Garden" (*Pencil Points,* 1938), 33, *34,* 41, 226n74

Freeman house (Frank Lloyd Wright), 42

Furlong, Ethelbert, 108

furniture: rebuilding of original, 211, *211,* 229n15; Rose design of, 10, 59, 83,117, 140, 190, *192;* in Rose garden and house, 107-8, 116-18, *117,* 161, 229n15

Gabo, Naum, 19; *Construction Spherique, 33*

Garden of Water and Light (Guevrekian), 24, *25*

"Gardens" (*California Arts and Architecture,* 1940), 91

gardens: awareness of change in, 83-84; conservation of existing features, 10, 77-78; environmentally sensitive nature of, 11; flexibility of spaces, 83; improvisation in, 9, 39, 68; as "space-sculpture," 5, 9, 10, 41, 61, 63, 81, 83, 147, 225n67; spatial experience of, 56, 60, 62, 66, 83; spatial geometry ("space-form"), 10, *53,* 60, 64, 93, 97, 99, 111, 120, 140, 159, 185, 192, *192,* 201, *203, 204;* spiritual and ecological

nature of, 6, 58, 74, 85; use of found objects in, 9-10, 49, 59-60, 118

Gardens in the Modern Landscape (1938), 223n36, 227-28n8

Gardens Make Me Laugh (1965), 9; comparison of Japanese and Western attitudes, 64, 65, 118, 222n9, 226n81

Gear, Charles, 148

General Signals (Stamford CT), corporate commission, 230n1

geometry. *See* gardens: spatial geometry

Germano garden (Saddle River NJ), *81*

Giedion, Sigfried, 31

Giedion-Welcker, Carola, 33

Gillmor, Jean (sister), 15, 47, 71 101, 103, 159-61, 230n3

Glickman garden (Allendale, NJ), 199-200; choreography of movement through, 197, 201-2, 205; collaboration with Eleanor Pettersen, 200; condition of, 206-7; dry streambed, 201-2, *203,* 205-6; outdoor living–dining room, 205; "rock ikebana," 205; use of rocks on site, 82, 201

Goldfinger, Erno, 223-24n40

Great Depression, 15, 43

Great Neck (NY), modular garden in, *54*

grid, the: joining outdoors and indoors, 107; in paving, 94, 101; use of, 83, 93, 111, 116, 120

Gropius, Walter, 31; as founder of Bauhaus, 24, 223n26; at Harvard, 40; as proponent of modern architecture, 30

of *Architectural Record* essays, 8, 221n4; trio with Rose and Eckbo, 3, 25, 26, 30-31, 221n3; understanding of space as key modern quality, 27, 223n40

Kings Point (NY), garden commission, 225n67

Klaiman garden (Saddle River, NJ): rock assemblage, *12;* "dry stream," *65*

Krakauer and Rosen garden: collaboration with Raymond, 225n67; first use of railroad ties, 225–26n73

Kral, Ken, 216

Krolewski, Karen, and James Rose Garden Documentation Project, 214

Ladies' Home Journal: articles in, 52; commission from, 227n3

lanai, in Averett garden, 140, *141, 142*

landscape architecture: modern revolution in, 8, 18, 27, 68; as practiced at Harvard, 29-31, 36; in relation to other arts, 35, 39, 41, 107; Rose's influence on profession, 3, 5-6, 8, 104; space as modernist focus, 26, 27, 223-24n40. *See also* Harvard Graduate School of Design; James Rose Center for Landscape Architectural Research and Design

Landscape Architecture: Fletcher Steele article, 26; review of *Modern American Gardens,* 38

Landscape for Living (Eckbo), 52

Landscape Forms, and adaptaton of bench design, 229n15

"Landscape Models" (*Pencil Points,* 1939), 37, 221n4; 224n45, 47

landscape space: attuned to needs of modern people, 27, 32; early writings on, 8; modern expression of, 9, 35. *See also* gardens

lanterns: description, 152, *152;* recycled materials, 10, 59, 147, *148,* 155, 157, 162; stone, 82, 185, *187*

Lapkin garden (Montvale NJ), 225n67

Leary, Timothy, 5

Levin, Kim, on experimental nature of modern art, 16, 222n17

Le Corbusier, Rose opinion of approach, 22–23

Linn, Karl, critique of Macht garden, 131

Lipchitz, Jacques, 225n67

Long Island (NY), white stones imported from, 193, 201

Macht garden and house (Baltimore, MD), *59,* 120, 121-32; concrete and blacktop paving, 82; existing trees as determinants of form, 79; *House and Garden* "Hallmark" award, 132; house and garden as integrated whole, 61, 122, 131, 225n67; terraces, 131

Macht, Lois, 121; description of Rose, 130; discussion with author, 229n1; recollections of project, 129-30

Macht, Philip, 121

Maloney garden (Saddle River NJ), *76*

Mallet-Stevens, Robert, 25

Manshu-in (Kyoto, Japan), example of dry stream, 232n2

Mariana Islands, naval service in, 45, 49

Mason, Bruce, 216

Matamoras (PA): family home in, 43, 47; birthplace, 186

McCall's, articles in, 52

Metuchen (NJ), garden commission, 225n67

Meyer, Elizabeth K.: on Rose house, 13; letter to ASLA Classic Award Jury, 222n10

Miami (FL), garden commission, 225n67

Michael Van Valkenburgh Associates: collaboration with James Rose Center, 229n15

Mineola (NY), garden, *10*

models: at Harvard, 33; at James Rose Center, 216; limitations of, 37-38, 225n69; use of, 8, 35, 37-38, 68, 93

Modern American Gardens— Designed by James Rose (1967): abstract ground plane elements, *150;* "caption story," 68, 148, 150; 155; changing essence of landscape design, 118-19, *149;* cynical tone of, 44; *67;* Marc Snow pseudonym, 30, 69; model making, 37; mosaic approach to bookmaking, 72; use of photographs, 68; publication, 118; purpose, 67-68; review of, 38; scene at Harvard in, 30, 40, 221n3

Prairie style, 20. *See also* Jensen, Jens; Wright, Frank Lloyd

Progressive Architecture: comparison of MoMA Japanese garden and Rose home, 108, *109, 110,* 111; "Houses and Landscapes," 131; modular landscape designs, 227n3; postwar essays, 52, 118; series of essays for, 8, 228n8. See also *Pencil Points*

Radcliffe, Donald, 122

railroad ties: in Averett garden, 140, 145; early use, 59, 60, 225–26n73; development of space-form with, 60–61; later use in benches and other features, 59, 82–83; Lois Macht on use of, 130; in Paley garden, 174–75, 179; replacement of with landscape timbers, 232n4; as scavenged material, 10, 60, 120

Rappaport, Lawrence, 227n106

Rasmussen, Meg, caretaker of James Rose Center, 210-11, 15

Raymond, Antonin: friend and mentor, 43; professional practice, 43–44, 224n5; Rose employer, 43–44, 108; and Rose exposure to Japanese culture, 222n8, 224n56

recycled materials: use of, 10, 151; at Averett garden, 140; at Macht garden, *59,* 129, 132; at Rose garden, 120

Ridgewood (NJ), description of, 228n1. *See also* Rose garden and house

Rieger, Charles, axonometric drawings by, 100, *100, 110,* 131, 225n69

Rigolo, Arthur, 74

River of Hospitality (mural), 232n2; restoration of, 212-3, *213*

"rock ikebana": at Anisfield garden, 185; as gateway, at Glickman garden, 202, 205; at Paley garden, 82, 179, *181;* at Rose garden and house, *165,* 171; use of found boulders in, 82

rocks: assemblages of, *12;* found on-site, 82, 171, *172,* 182, 201; redeployment of, 80; reuse of, 78. *See also* stones

Rose, Clarence (father), 15, 222n14

Rose garden and house (Ridgewood, NJ), *7, 23, 105,* 103-20, 159-72, 208-19; conflicts with building inspector, 73, 103, 163; constant reinvention of, 13, 71, 85, 104, 117-18, 120, 159, 162-63, 171; deterioration of, 171, 210-12, 214; flexible design of, 106, 116; integrated spatial character of, 104, 107, 111, 114-15, 168; in *Progressive Architecture,* 108; renovation of, 69, 159, 162, 214-16, 232n2; as Zen study center, 71, 159, 165-67. *See also* James Rose Center for Landscape Architectural Research and Design; zendo

Rose, James

—early life, 14-15, 29

—education: enrollment at Cornell, 5; expulsion from Harvard, 5, 32-33; failure to graduate from high school, 5; student with Eckbo and Kiley, 3, 8, 25, 26, 30-31, 221n3, 223n40

—military experience: basic training, 44; disillusionment caused by, 45-46, 50-51; letters to mother while serving, 69; private world created in response to, 45-47, 49, 85, 105

—personal views and characteristics: creativity, 45, 47-50, 54-56, 58-59, 66, 73-74, 77, 85-86; difficult personality, 5, 11, 13, 66-67, 74, 80-81, 130, 163-64, 195; frugality, 49, 59, 81,85, 120,197; interest in theater, 18-19, 30, 42, 72, 222-23n19; rebellious nature, 3, 8, 18, 27, 87; resistance to authority, 33, 46-47, 49-50, 52, 54, 66, 86, 113; social criticism, 5, 9, 32-33, 41, 52, 55, 86; spiritual quest, 58, 62, 65-66, 74, 84-86, 167,193, 222n13; and Zen Buddhism, 5, 65-66, 71, 72, 159, 165, 167, 222n13

—professional life: effort to establish West Coast practice, 42; employed by Antonin Raymond, 43, 108; Lower West Side office, 51; Eleanore Pettersen's description of, 52; postwar career, 52; teaching, 52, 225n69

—professional philosophy: appreciation of Japanese culture, 11, 63-66, 108, 186, 197, 205, 222n8,